ALISTAIR MACLEOD

ESSAYS ON HIS WORKS

WRITERS SERIES 8

SERIES EDITORS:
ANTONIO D'ALFONSO AND JOSEPH PIVATO

Guernica Editions Inc. acknowledges the support of
The Canada Council for the Arts.
Guernica Editions Inc. acknowledges the support of
the Ontario Arts Council.
Guernica Editions Inc. acknowledges the financial support of
the Government of Canada through the Book Publishing
Industry Development Program (BPIDP).

ALISTAIR MACLEOD

ESSAYS ON HIS WORKS

EDITED BY IRENE GUILFORD

GUERNICA
TORONTO·BUFFALO·LANCASTER (U.K.)
2001

Irene Guilford, editor
Guernica Editions Inc.
P.O. Box 117, Station P, Toronto (ON), Canada M5S 2S6
2250 Military Road, Tonawanda, N.Y. 14150-6000 U.S.A.
Gazelle, Falcon House, Queen Sq., Lancaster LA1 1RN U.K.

Typeset by Selina.
Printed in Canada.
First edition.

Legal Deposit — Third Quarter
National Library of Canada
Library of Congress Catalog Card Number: 2001095240
National Library of Canada Cataloguing in Publication Data
Main entry under title:
Alistair MacLeod : essays on his works
(Writers series ; 8)
Includes bibliographical references.
ISBN 1-55071-137-7

1. MacLeod, Alistair – Criticism and interpretation.
I. Guilford, Irene. II Series: Writers series (Toronto, Ont.) ; 8
PS8575.L459Z553 2001   C813'.54   C2001-902457-6
PR9199.3.M3342Z553 2001

Contents

Acknowledgements

"The Vision of Alistair MacLeod" by Jane Urquhart is reprinted with the kind permission of McClelland & Stewart. A portion of "Alligators in the Sewers" by Douglas Gibson appeared in *The National Post*.

Introduction

IRENE GUILFORD

In Alistair MacLeod's novel, *No Great Mischief*, there is a scene between the young dental student Alexander and his professor. They are having a drink in a bar. The young student, nervous and anxious in the company of the older man, has neither the money to buy his share of the beer, nor the desire to drink, as he wishes to study for his exams. He switches to coke. As the older man continues to drink, they talk. Finally, the professor, in his cups, asks,

> "Where did you say you come from?"
> "Oh," I said, startled by the simplicity or complexity of the question. "From Cape Breton."

This scene raises a situation familiar to many Canadians. Where do you come from? It is a question that can be answered as simply as, "I am from Cape Breton," or with the more complex response, "Yes, but I am of the old country too," an answer bringing with it a particular mindset of preoccupations, a set of concerns carrying complex emotional weight, like an aura. This connection is one that many of Alistair MacLeod's characters feel, a tie so strong and pervasive that when the sister in *No Great Mischief* has occasion to visit Scotland, even though she has never been there before, she is immediately recognized by the locals as one of their own. It is part of everyday, ordinary life, a connection spoken of and maintained between brother and sister in *No Great Mischief* during the brother's visit to his sister's house in Calgary, or constantly referred to when Alexander visits his brother Calum in Toronto, the subject leaping into conversation immediately, as if it is the one, the only subject of importance. And in the background, there is the constant talk of grandparents, like a gentle murmuring, Grandpa with his lively and fun-loving stories, Grandfather with his more sober reading of history books, Grandma with her sayings, a guiding family presence that wraps around the characters like mist.

It starts with a sense of exile, a mood of lamentation and longing, a looking back that can last for generations. There is the sense of two worlds, the complexity of departure and return, as in "The Vastness of the Dark," "The Lost Salt Gift of Blood," and "The Return." Education can be seen as both an opportunity for betterment and a potential force of separation from family, culture and clan, as in "The Golden Gift of Grey." Grandparents are enormous presences, always strong and loving custodians, but also carriers of culture, brought to their zenith in *No Great Mischief* as creatures hovering on the twilight fringes of myth. There is loyalty to the clan, as the young Alexander learns when it becomes his turn, upon the death of his cousin at the bottom of the mine, to step in to take his place in the mining gang that is *clann Chalum Ruaidh*. There is the constant presence of the past, through history and story, myth and song, an influence so deep that it lasts for life. And, as the old man in "Clearances" demonstrates, there is history, an inescapable, repetitive tide.

And of course, there is language, a force laid down early and emotionally potent. Whether it be Gaelic or Italian, French or Lithuanian, it is a stamp on the heart, affecting the way we think and view the world, what we dream and hold dear. Whether we speak it amongst ourselves, as in "The Closing Down of Summer," hear it spoken around us, or only hear the echoes from distant generations, somehow it rests within us, perhaps hidden so deeply as to be out of sight, but still underground, a river that can pour forth, as the sister who goes to Scotland in *No Great Mischief* discovers. Perhaps no one puts it better than Alistair Macleod himself. "The language you grow up with is the language of your heart."

The essays in this book explore the hold on the heart that is Alistair MacLeod's writing. Jane Urquhart speaks of the intensity, the depth and the breadth of the vision. Janice Kulyk Keefer writes of the dignity of labour and its influence on people's lives. David Williams explores clan and oral culture. Colin Nicholson shows us how history, legend, storytelling, memory and myth can contribute to identity. Karl Jirgens follows the circular nature of the narrative and the cycle of flux captured in MacLeod's work. Douglas Gibson gives us a glimpse into the writer/publisher relationship that led to the publication of *No Great Mischief*. And Shelagh Rogers journeyed to Cape Breton to interview Alistair MacLeod in his home, giving us the writer and the man.

How do we become who we are? How do we live in the present and move forward into the future without losing intimacy with our country of origin and our past, our emotional island? How do we keep the faith and maintain loyalty? These questions are MacLeod territory.

As Canadians, we all grapple with them, to some degree or another, at some point in our lives. It makes no difference whether we hail from the British Isles, Eastern or Southern Europe, China or India, the South Pacific, the Caribbean or Latin America, whether we are recent immigrants or from a generation long established, whether we have left our point of origin irrevocably behind, or still have strong ties back home. As we make our homes, here, in this beautiful country, we also settle down, somewhere, along this uneasy spectrum.

And yet Alistair MacLeod challenges us to go further, to take one step back, to look beyond our own borders to the greater world at large. As the migrant workers in *No Great Mischief* attest, migration and displacement are no longer occasional concerns, intermittent disruptions of history, but rather, constant and steady streams. What do we have in common? What do we share? What can we know, within the limits of human understanding, about one another? This is writing that nudges one towards that most complex and wondrous state of being – an individual rooted in personal history and locale, connected to the past, but also a citizen of the world, a person who would try to understand why Zulus dance. Where do we come from? Alistair MacLeod's birthplace is Canadian, his emotional heartland Cape Breton, his heritage Scottish, but his writing is of the world.

An Interview with Alistair MacLeod

SHELAGH ROGERS

Shelagh Rogers: 2000 has been a great year for you. You've won the Trillium Award, The Canadian Booksellers Association Award for Book of the Year. Closer to your Cape Breton home, there was the Thomas Raddall Prize for best novel by a writer from Nova Scotia and now, practically right in your own home, the Broad Cove Parish prize. What does it mean to you to be so honoured by your people, here?

AM: Oh, it's nice to be honoured by the people here. This is where I grew up. And as far as the annual Broad Cove Concert is concerned, I was there at the first one, forty-four years ago. And I've continued to work with the Broad Cove concert . . . to take tickets and to do things that people from other households do and it was very nice to be so honoured by them. This dispels the idea that you never profit in your hometown. I don't know that most people around here would consider me a prophet, but they expressed their appreciation in a very loving way, I felt.

SR: Part of the prize was a painting of your house, which I'm staring at right now. White wooden house on a green hill, blue sky. It's a lovely tribute.

AM: They gave me a painting of my house, yes. It's very nice of them and I appreciate it a great deal.

SR: You are from here, but you weren't born here. It was North Battleford, Saskatchewan. And you came here when you were how old, ten or so?

AM: Ten, yes. The house that we're in is my great-grand-father's house. He's the austere gentleman with the whiskers up there in that photo on the wall. He was born in 1838 and he built this house. And although I was not born in this house, this is the house that my father was born in and this is also the house that my grandfather was born in. They were born at a time prior to hospitals, so people were actually born in their own homes. So I am quite satisfied to be still here in my great-grandfather's house.

SR: You grew up in a mining family. There's a long lineage of miners. When was it that you knew you wanted to be a writer?

AM: I always liked going to school and I always liked literature and I always liked to read and I always liked to write. And I was the kind of person who won the English prize in grade twelve, that type of thing. But I never thought of it as a career. And I suppose now the full realization of it as a career is coming at sixty-four years of age. So this is hardly a child prodigy to whom you are speaking. But I thought of it as the way somebody who can sing may think of their abilities, and say well, I can sing or I can catch a baseball but I don't think that I will ever make my living at it. And I haven't made my living at it. I made my living basically as a university professor. But I always liked to write and I think I began to take it seriously when I went to the United States. I went to the United States to study for a Ph.D. and one of the things that you do when you study for a Ph.D. in English is you read and you analyze stories and various kinds of literature. And as I was reading all of these stories and analyzing them, I began to think maybe I could write some of these stories instead of just analyzing other people's stories all the time.

And I was six years in the United States. I was removed, I suppose, from this landscape. I had worked away, but I was always back and forth on weekends and so on, so it was as if I had never left here. But when I went to the United States I really left physically, if not emotionally or intellectually. And I began to think of this landscape in a kind of objective or in a kind of distant manner. And I became, I think, more thoughtful about it. It's like living in a house with your parents and you just take them for granted. And then when you go away, or twenty years later, you say, oh, I didn't realize how much work my mother did or I never realized a lot of these things when I was ten or twenty. But now that I'm thirty, I think of them in a different way.

So those two factors combined to make me begin to write my own work. The fact that I was absent from my native landscape, shall we call it, and the fact that I was analyzing literature and thinking about literature. And I went to the University of Notre Dame because there was quite a splendid creative writing teacher there at the time: a man named Frank O'Malley and he taught Edwin O'Connor who wrote *The Last Hurrah*. I was looking at all of these piles of applications that you get from various grad schools. I talked to different people and a lot of different people said this would be a good place for you to go rather than the University of Chicago or the University of Toronto or the University of Texas and so on. So I took their advice and I went there and it was a very good place, I thought, because it was interested in the creation of literature, in addition to the criticism of literature. So I think I was quite fortunate that happened to me, that I just didn't sit in the carrel all day analyzing the works of other people. That would be my life had I not gone to a kind of creative, imaginative university.

SR: Along the way, though, you did also work in the mines.

AM: Yes, I went to university working in the mines. My father was a miner and my grandfather was a miner and nearly all of the people from this area were involved in mining of one kind or another and a lot of us still are. My brother-in-law is currently a miner in northern Manitoba.

SR: So it's still in the family. You have also worked as a logger, right?

AM: Yes, I worked in a logging camp. I worked at the North end of Vancouver Island. I was quite young and I was quite athletic at the time and it was not a very good job. They couldn't keep anybody in this particular camp but I was so far from home I had to stay. And I ended up being promoted to second rigger – the person who aligns the spire trees –because I was able to climb the hill and then climb the mountain and then climb the spire tree so I rose rapidly through the logging profession.

SR: Literally! What kept you working as a logger at that time?

AM: It was mainly that no one else would stay to do this work. And I remember when I left (this happened several times, when I left the logging camp . . .), they said, "you're making a big mistake MacLeod. You know you better stay here." The spire trees could have been my life. So yes, I did that, all of that. I never minded, and when I worked in a mine, I never minded that. I think I was probably schooled in such a way as to be grateful to have these jobs. I was not of the society of complaint. So I never minded any of these jobs.

SR: You say you were athletic at the time. This physical world of logging and fishing and mining has really permeated your stories. In "The Closing Down of Summer," one of the characters talks about what he'd like to tell his wife and children about what he does . . . about "the beauty of motion on the edge of violence," I think, is how he puts it.

AM: Well, one of the things about working in the mine or even working in the logging camps is that nobody sees what you do except your fellow workers. And the Scottish poet Andrew Greig once said something to me in reference to mountain climbers. He said, "Mountain climbers are athletes without fans." They are way up there in the sky and nobody knows what they are doing except the other mountain climbers who happen to be with them and they are all sort of dependent on one another lest they might fall. And nobody knows how good they are and they better not be bad or they will die up in the sky, up above the clouds. I think mining is somewhat the same. Nobody knows what miners do except other miners and to be a successful miner you almost always have to be big because it's big heavy work.

There are small men that work in the mine the same way there are small men who play in the NFL or in the Canadian Football League but it is kind of a profession, let's say, that depends on physical strength.

And in terms of the local area here, my father's bones were calcified. He got lead poisoning in Virginia City, Nevada and he almost died. Another of his brothers who stayed here lost an eye in a mine and another one lost a hand, and a fourth one broke a leg. So all this is the idea that when you go out to work you may come back if not minus your life, minus your arm or minus your eye or minus your toes or something like that, this is something to think about. Because if you lose your eye, or you lose your hand, your life is then forever changed, especially if you are involved in physical work. It's not like being an accountant or university professor or a radio announcer or a real-estate salesman or a lot of jobs where perhaps you don't need your body for the fulfillment of your career. It's interesting, because everybody has stress and everybody worries and all of the rest of it. But I think the cliché is that people who do physical work are not as smart as those who do sedentary things but I don't think this is true. I think in that physical world that I just described, you worry a lot because, say, if I lose my foot today or if this rock comes down on my foot, or on my head, if I don't lose my life, my life will be forever changed. And in the same way, those who depend upon me, their lives will be different if they have a crippled father. So I think it's something to think about and to consider.

SR: These are men who are articulate in a different way.

AM: Yes, articulate in a different way. The image that I

had in "The Closing Down of Summer," although it doesn't appear at all in the story, was of Howard Cosel interviewing these great basketball players and they would do these ballet-like things. And then he would say to them that question that interviewers ask athletes, "What's going through your mind, Tom, when you're driving to the basket?" And then you would show a close-up of them doing this and they would look at themselves. They'd be kind of astounded at seeing themselves doing these things and they would say things like "I just shoot the ball," because they weren't comfortable. And I thought here is an almost completely physical man talking to an almost completely verbal man, and neither of them could do what the other can do.

But what I liked about that image was that if you do this on TV, you don't have to talk about it because it's like show and tell. If you can't tell, I'll say, well, I'll show you how to slam-dunk the basketball. But for people in the mines or the mountain climbers or people like that, they are not on TV. And so they have to try to explain the nature of their lives to those whom they love. They have to fall back on words. And I think being fully articulate is probably a kind of acquired skill. And a lot of people down in the mine hardly ever talk because there is so much noise. They just make hand signals and they gesture when they want the heavy machinery closer to them or farther away from them.

So they live in a silence. And the other thing is, especially in hard rock mines, that a lot of them become deaf because of the hammering of the steel on the stone. And if you have ever been around deaf people, when they talk to each other, they understand one another. Sometimes they talk loudly and sometimes they understand one another through lip reading. They almost see the sound rather than hear it. It's a kind of transfer of the senses. So all of those things were the kind of ideas that I thought were worthwhile exploring in "The Closing Down of Summer" and in other stories as well.

SR: There is so much at stake . . . that kind of enormous risk in this hard, physical world. How conscious of that are the men as they go off to work everyday?

AM: Some are and some are not, I think. Again I make the analogy of people who play professional hockey for a living and people who play football. Big men who are two hundred and forty pounds, who are kind of on the edge of violence, are kind of graceful and beautiful. But it's hard physical work and I think that within that group you find all kinds of very thoughtful people. And then you may find people who are not so thoughtful. I think like in all areas of work, some people think a lot about what they do everyday and think is this worthwhile or is this how I should spend my time. Or should I get out of this before I'm too old, or should I take a course in computer technology or whatever. I think people who go to work, regardless of their occupation, are quite thoughtful about it and other people just go and they're too busy for thought or they don't want to think about it or they are not inclined in that way.

SR: Even though these men are working in teams, so often, as you say, they can't hear each other. A fisherman might call to his buddy in the back of the boat and his voice will be lost in the wind. I guess there has to be great individual responsibility.

AM: Yes, there's a great deal of individual responsibility. But the other side of it, as you mentioned, is that they do work in teams. If you're out in the boat and you don't have somebody with you who can jump around and pull the anchor or do what he's supposed to do at the right time, you are in trouble. So people are, I think, if they can be, careful about those to whom they are forced to entrust their lives. I think this is why certain crews are careful. They would say well, I don't necessarily want him because he's clumsy or he's hung over or he's irresponsible or something like that. And I think the same is true in the fishing boats. That people who are in fishing boats around here, they know what they are doing. I mean, they have to know what they are doing. And very often they are uncles or nephews or fathers and sons or brothers which means that there is a relationship that exists outside of the boat that may exist within their homes or within their communities.

SR: Is it lonely work?

AM: No, I don't think it's lonely. I know when they closed the mines in Cape Breton here a lot of the men said that they missed the camaraderie because it's an all male world. That's probably not highly recommended but it's a physical world and it's an all male world in a lot of the old Celtic communities and the same was true here. If women went down in the mine or even went near it, it was considered bad luck. Which I guess is a step up from those stories from the Welsh mines where the women were down in harnesses pulling the boxes. But I think, in an all male situation, there is probably a lot of horsing around or a lot of camaraderie and so on. And it's interesting that this, when the mines closed in Cape Breton, that this is what so many of the men say that they missed.

SR: The hero in your novel *No Great Mischief*, though he works with drills and with picks, is not a miner. He is an orthodontist. Why did you decide to give him this profession?

AM: Well, I wanted a modern man, a modern character. And a hundred years ago I don't think there was such a thing as an orthodontist. I wanted a kind of very modern profession and I wanted my man to be rich. And I liked the idea of what the orthodontist does is improves teeth and jaw lines. And he makes people better on the outside but the people still may be rats on the inside. So it's a cosmetic kind of profession and the world could get along, I think, without an orthodontist in it. Probably the world could not get along or quite so well without a dentist or without a doctor. But I thought it was the kind of profession that appeals to vanity and people are willing to pay for vanity.

So I see this man, who thinks it might be nice to be rich. And when he's in medical school, in Halifax, his professor says if you want to get rich you better get out of here, because the Atlantic area is not an area in which people pay a lot of attention to their teeth. Nor do they in Quebec and so on. So you have to go wherever teeth are kind of a priority to people. So he says okay and he goes to Southern Ontario where a lot of people care about their teeth and will pay a lot of money. But not as much money as if he were to go to Texas, where there are more rich people who care even more about their teeth.

The other side of that, though, is that it is a profession

that makes people feel better about themselves and gives them confidence and so on. And it's also, as you mentioned, a kind of pick and drill operation where you wear latex gloves in the fulfilling of your destiny. So I thought it was a great profession to give my central character and personally allowed me to read a lot of magazines that dentists read.

SR: I want to ask you about memory. There's a point where Alexander, the orthodontist, is asked by his older brother Calum whether he remembers their parents. And he says he's not sure how many of his memories are real and how many he's made up from other people's stories. What do you think memories are made of?

AM: I think in the novel what I liked about these people, about the twins, Alexander and Catherine, was that their parents die when they are so young that they never really know them. They don't remember them as real people. When you're sixteen your father and mother are real people but if your parents are taken from you when you're three, maybe you idolize them. Maybe you idealize them almost too much. You sort of say, "oh, my mother would never make me clean my ears" or a lot of little things like that because you didn't know them as people.

Between Calum and Alexander and his twin sister, there are thirteen years . . . a lot of time in a life of a child. Between thirty-three and forty-six, it may not be. When you are fully formed as an adult, that gap may not be so great. But if you are three and people are always saying to you "oh, you should have known your mother, oh, you should have known your father," then you make them up in terms of what others have given to you in their conversations.

Calum, the older brother, remembers their father and remembers their mother. I think that in Calum's memory of the parents, they're like real people. He remembers his father's skills or his mother's interests and so on. But for these younger people, they don't remember them at all. And this is why they are always looking at the photograph albums because that's sort of all they have . . . pictures. Both the physical pictures that they look at in the album, or the pictures they recreate about themselves and about their parents are kind of imaginary. I have that theme all through the novel. You know the more serious grandfather, because he was born out wedlock . . .

SR: He was a "come by chance"? Is that what it was called?

AM: Yes, come by chance is a phrase they used to use. Well, because he never saw his own father, and didn't have a picture of him, he looks at himself in the mirror and tries to recreate this absentee dead father by looking backwards. Rather than saying the children look like their parents, he's trying to make the parent look like him. And I think this idea of understanding where you came from is a central one within the novel. And this is why Alexander then starts reading all of this Scottish history.

He starts out trying to understand where he came from physically himself. Then he goes backward or forward, backward or forward trying to understand where we all came from. And it becomes very murky, as all of these explorations do. It's like modern day people who have been adopted trying to now look for their real biological parents and who knows what they may find there. They may be wonderful people or you may say oh, I wish I had never found them. They may not always be up to your ideals or what you would want them to be. They may just be people who may be connected to you by blood but may not be very much like you at all.

So that was what I trying to do with the twins . . . trying to imagine their parents. And the grandfather trying to imagine his parents. And then fiddling around with Scottish history as it interacts with French history or British history. I think of the cheerful grandfather who just runs around saying all MacDonalds are good and they never make mistakes. You know, this is a simpler view of the world, which is great – right? But the other grandfather is always saying, "oh, I don't think we're that great" or "you should look at this." He says, "I don't want to hear that." It's like the story of the king of the herring. It's such a great story, this herring that's leading all the other herring towards us so we could eat them. The other side says, "well, he's really betraying his herring followers" and he says, "oh, I don't want to think of that." There are some issues that are solved much more simply and others that . . . you will never find answers to them, perhaps.

SR: About remembrance and imagining the past, do you think you can remember past events that never happened to you? Can you remember events that you've never seen or experienced . . .

AM: I think you can. But the thing is, can you remember them accurately. If you say this is the way I choose to remember things, or this is the way I choose to view things, this is very prevalent in the modern world. If you say well here is land and you talk to Israeli people about this land and you talk to Palestinian people about this land and you talk to ethnic Albanians and you talk to Serbians and you say now this is our land, and they say no, no. This is our land. I think these issues are just part of the human condition wherever people are at odds and are very, very certain in their beliefs.

I wrote the novel with the idea of exploring belief because I think it's very interesting. You say how can you people on this side of the fence believe this and the people on the other side believe totally the opposite? The answer is it's easy because we're who we are and they're who they are, so why don't you all shake hands? Well, it's not so easy because in the modern world in the novel people are carrying history within them and they are not at all instant people who just say history began at my birth and that's all there is to it. Because to a lot of people that's not all there is to it at all. And I was interested in the idea that once you know things, you can't forget them until Alzheimer's strikes or something like that.

SR: You can't not know or unknow what you know. You mentioned Israel and that makes me think about a place where ancient language is being preserved as the language of the state. I was just reading an article as we were driving here about lost languages. There's an American linguist who thinks that about three thousand languages will vanish in the next century.

AM: Yeah, there are some other statistics that say there is one language lost every day or something. I read somewhere or somebody told me that eighty percent of the messages on the Internet are in English which is interesting. I guess why I'm talking about the Internet, about which I know very little, is the fact that it represents progress. And it's very, very hard to stand in the way of progress. And I think for the Gaelic-speaking people, English was the language of progress. In order to be progressive, in order to get a job, you have to learn the majority language, especially if you go to work for other people. You could work on a fishing boat and you could work maybe in a mine. You could work in the woods as long as you worked by yourself. But if you were a unilingual Gaelic speaker today and you went to Halifax or you went to Toronto, goodness help you. You would be lucky to get a job scrubbing floors. You wouldn't be able to speak your native language.

So this is the tension. I think this is the tension in Quebec. How can we preserve our language and our culture and our beliefs and so on while still being part of the year 2000. I mean, you can't say "but we're never going to go to the Internet, we're not going to become computer literate" because then you will be left behind. But I think the issue there, and it's the issue with people who are interested in language, is how can you retain the language while living in a dominant culture which does not use your language? It would be nice. It is quite amazing to go to Europe and see people who speak four languages, like in Switzerland, where everybody speaks four languages and gets along fine. But in Britain and in North America and in Australia and wherever English is spoken it seems to be a big unilingual community.

I'm interested when I go abroad and encounter people from Norway or people from Finland, reasonably small countries, who say to me you are very lucky that you write in English because you have this big audience who can read you without effort. If you are a writer in Finland or maybe even in a bigger country like Italy, to get whatever you wish to say out to the larger world, you have to be translated and translation is expensive and it's long. And maybe they won't translate it in such a way that what you are saying is really what they're receiving.

Now in terms of wars, I think that it's easier to kill people if they speak a language that is different than yours. Then they're more "the other" as we say. And we don't know what they're saying and so they become, I wouldn't say less human than you are, but different. And I think this is what is interesting about the American Revolution or the American Civil War, that people spoke the same language. And, you know, you don't want to kill your relative. They would think about that, whereas if you're speaking Gaelic or Irish, which is the same language, referred to as the Irish tongue, they were very often said to be speaking gibberish because the English would not understand them. I think, say, in the conquering of North America, who knows what was in the Cree heart or the Apache heart because they spoke another kind of language.

SR: I guess it made General Wolfe's job easier on the Plains of Abraham to send the Highlanders, who not only spoke Gaelic but sometimes spoke French as well, out onto the field as fodder.

AM: I think that General Wolfe had these people and he was uncomfortable with them because they would speak languages that he couldn't speak. And he had fought against them and I think when you fight against people and then suddenly they're fighting with you, you're not sure what animosities exist. I think that I have sympathy for General Wolfe. I think that he was a good General and he was given a job. And he was given certain people with whom to do this job, and I think that he felt more uncomfortable with some than he did with others. I think he was given a job and maybe he didn't like them and maybe they didn't like him. Maybe some of them did and some of them didn't but I think it's probably more complicated than it might appear at first.

After the novel was out, a Francophone scholar gave me a note that he found from Montcalm. And Montcalm was saying if only we could get these fellows, the Highlanders, on our side. I think by that time a lot of the Highlanders had become sort of mercenary. They would fight on one side or they might fight on the other side. I'm interested in that idea. Maybe a lot of them were fighting with their heart and maybe they weren't either. They were kind of conscripted, some of them.

Then afterwards I think it's, again, maybe like professional athletes who really like playing for the Montreal Canadiens and then they get traded to the Boston Bruins or Philadelphia. And they say I don't like playing for them so much but I'll play, I get paid. So your heart may not always be in your work and you still may be able to do your work very well. But for other people their heart or their love really is in what they're doing. Maybe just to look at people you can't say well your heart's in your work and I don't think yours is. I think it's interesting.

SR: I have a picture in my mind that comes from your writing about the American Revolution where Gaelic speakers fought on both sides. And that they would sing to each other at night and try and call each other over to their side through song. Is that true?

AM: Yes, that's very interesting because they were again known as sort of mercenary and some of them became Americans. In the Carolinas, those areas are full of Highlanders today, lots of MacDonalds and lots of other people as well. Their songs are interesting because they were singing to the people who were fighting on the British side. The future is here and you were treated badly by the British anyway and why don't you come over and start a new life in America . . . this is really going to work.

The other people were singing songs of no it's not going to work, come over on the side of King George or whatever, and all will be forgiven and you can go back to the Highlands and you will get a strip of land. It's kind of like Tokyo Rose. They were singing to one another but the English-speaking people again who were the equivalent of General Wolfe would not know what they were saying. They were singing back and forth, singing across these valleys at night, singing Gaelic songs and there are some of them in fact who expressed these sentiments on both sides.

SR: There's a line that you quote in your novel from Margaret Laurence's *The Diviners* where Morag talks about lost languages lurking inside the ventricles of the heart. And Catherine, who is Alexander's twin, talks about Gaelic as a subterranean river running deep inside her. How true is that for you?

AM: It doesn't run very deeply in me because I'm not fluent enough in the language. But I think of the characters as fluent in the language. I'm not a fluent Gaelic speaker. I understand some words. My wife, on the other hand, is a fluent Gaelic speaker. She can write it, read it and sing it. She grew up in a house two miles from the house you are sitting in now and I think that the difference is that in her house there were people who were unilingual Gaelic speakers longer than there were perhaps unilingual Gaelic speakers in this house. And I think in this community there are houses where there are lots of Gaelic speakers and then their next door neighbours with the same name, let's say the ubiquitous MacDonalds, who have lost the language.

In my wife's family, because she's the oldest in her family and they had a grandmother who was basically a Gaelic speaker and her friends were Gaelic speakers, there would be a lot of people who were speaking Gaelic at the time. And as a child you would just pick up whatever is around you. After the grandmother died and there's considerable age difference between my wife and her youngest brother, the youngest brother has practically no Gaelic at all but everybody in the house thinks he has because he's from that house. But he missed it. That's how fast it happens within one family. What I find interesting about the language is, I think your first language is the language of your heart, the language of your feelings. And then if you learn languages for your work, I don't think you learn emotional languages.

My grandparents who lived into their nineties both began as Gaelic speakers. And then my grandfather, who had to find work in a mine or something, he became an English speaker and then when he became old he reverted back to being a Gaelic speaker. My grandmother, because she didn't work out of the home, was more of a Gaelic speaker but I think the kind of English my Grandfather and men of his generation would have learned, they would learn words like *pick, ax, shovel*. But I don't think they would ever be able to say "I love you" in English because it would be too foreign. So I would say when they were in bed at night they would speak in Gaelic and then when he would go to work he would say "pass me the pick," or whatever, in English . . . I'm interested in that kind of idea because I think that for people like that, they were a Gaelic-speaking people 'til they were thirty and then they were English-speaking people until they were sixty and then they were Gaelic-speaking people again from sixty to ninety.

SR: Why do you think that is?

AM: I think they would be comfortable with it. You see, I think the language grafted onto them would be the language of utility or work.

SR: Alistair, there's a character I want you to talk about from one of your short stories. He's twenty-six and he knows he's going to die of cancer and he recalls more and more of the past as he has less and less of a future.

AM: Yes, this is from the story "The Road to Rankin's Point." If you go to the doctor and the doctor says you have six months to live then what will you do? As that character says, well, I'll do anything. If somebody said all these magic potions or somebody said go and stand under a certain tree for four days, or eat the leaves of the such and such . . . all of those are Highland remedies, he would do it because he wants to stay alive. But if that doesn't work, he has this death sentence and it's not like someone getting hit by a truck when we go out. He knows it's coming and then his idea is what will I do now because he has no future. He has four months of a future or six months. So then, given the kind of person he is, he goes back into the past because he has more past than he has a future.

And in those little scenes that I have there, he goes to visit the grandmother because he thinks, mistakenly, that the older the people are, the more they must know about death. In young persons' terminology, old people die and young people live. But that doesn't work either because the Grandmother is full of life and when he says well, I'm going to die at twenty-six, she says don't be so silly. Nobody dies at twenty-six, but he is going to die. And this is his reality although it's not anybody else's reality until the final scene of the story.

SR: A lot of your characters fall under the care of their grandparents or aunts and uncles but mostly grandparents. What is it that grandparents can give the child of their children?

AM: I think they can give them wisdom and experience because they've lived longer than the grandchildren or the children who are the current parents. And I think they may have values, they may have beliefs that are, I wouldn't say under attack, but maybe questioned in the year 2000 and very often those values might be good. The other thing that's interesting about grandparents is that they probably have more time than a lot of people. They have time to talk and they have time to interact with children. Whereas a lot of modern people are so busy running around, they perhaps don't have time. I think that if you have grandparents, it's a great gift because it allows you to see another way of life. And it allows you to have somebody else who loves you and cares about you who can show you certain things. Whether you accept all of these things or not, at least they are shown to you.

SR: In *No Great Mischief* there is an article in a magazine in an orthodontist's office, about the rearing of the modern child, an article that is really a warning about grandparents.

AM: Well, yes. Those articles exist, as you know. They're out there and they say this is what grandparents represent or what they don't represent . . . they don't love their grandchildren as much as they love their own children and so on. But all of this is questionable in the novel in terms of what the orthodontist knows about his own life.

SR: And he and his twin sister were raised by his grandparents.

AM: See, there is lots of information out there that clashes with a personal reality. It's like all red haired people have blue eyes. They don't.

SR: Or bad tempers.

AM: Or bad tempers. This is a cliché that follows people around. All Irishmen are drunk all of the time. Scotsmen are penny pinchers. All of these little national anvils that are hung on any ethnic group's neck that are not necessarily true.

SR: Right. Bad or good, they're sayings. What about the grandmother's sayings in *No Great Mischief*? She has a number of them. Rules to live by, including "always look after your own blood." That's the big artery, I guess, that runs through the novel . . . about family loyalty.

AM: The way I see her is she is a woman who really knows how to lead a life. It may not be the only way to lead a life. She is not impressed that this educated grandchild becomes an orthodontist, because it's too strange for her to understand. And then the granddaughter becomes an actress. She says to her "why don't you just be yourself?" This is the kind of dismissal of the acting profession that I wouldn't recommend, but she just sees things in very practical terms. A penny saved is a penny earned and I think that these maxims worked out just fine for her. If she says being an actress is a silly profession, well, in that area she's just wrong. You know, a lot of her statements don't apply to everybody. Grandma always used to say "you'll get used to anything except a nail in your shoe" and Calum, the older brother says well maybe this is a nail in my shoe but I'm not forgetting. I'm not getting used to this at all. Well, and maybe you won't. But I do like her. She's so certain. She really knows how to live a life and she lives to be over a hundred and she follows her rules. The issue may be a lot of things that your grandparents do for you and a lot of the advice they give you is very good. But still in the year 1980 or something, maybe her view of the world is not the only view that is to be followed or to be respected. "Always look after your own blood." She says "if I didn't believe that where would you two be?" This means, I think, she really has a grip upon those children. She says if I didn't believe that, you could have been sent to an orphanage or something like that. Not that they would ever do that to people in that time I don't think. "Always look after your own blood" is a maxim that is almost a threat. Calum does not feel this as deeply because he wasn't raised by the person with what borders upon a strong religious belief.

SR: A code.

AM: A code, but when Alexander says he says we have to do this, we have to look after our cousin, because Grandma says this, Calum says, okay you're doing it for Grandma. I'm doing it for you. And then, of course, this structure of the novel becomes again not as simple as "always look after your own blood." It becomes more complicated than they probably thought it was.

SR: There's a great scene where the grandmother's husband has had too much to drink and he topples spectacularly out of his chair and onto the floor. And she makes him into the reverse of a snow angel and puts Christmas decorations on him. And it's just such a beautiful scene.

AM: Well, I like both of those people, that set of grandparents because I think they are very happy, and with each other and everything. And I think that they probably contrast with the other Grandfather who is much more thoughtful. This doesn't mean that if you're happy, you're not thoughtful. And she does say about her husband, that he's smarter than some people think. Some people think that just because you're running around drinking beer or singing songs all of the time, that this is an indication of superficiality or something of that nature. But he's not a bit superficial. He's just a happy man and the other grandfather is a more thoughtful man. So, if you want somebody to sing songs, go to this grandfather. If you want someone to fill out your income tax, go to the other one. And of course the cheerful grandfather thinks of the other grandfather as a kind of a stick in the mud, although he is his best friend. And the other grandfather thinks of the grandpa figure as someone who spends hours playing cards and drinking beer and his view is that man should be doing something more worthwhile than just spending his time singing songs or whatever. The other grandfather knows the songs as well but he's more scholarly or interested in being clean or whatever his interests are. I think they're a nice contrast because they are related and they have the same name and they come from the same genetic background. They're not at all the same though. All MacDonalds are not the same.

SR: There's a nice thought in the novel about Robert Stanfield, the former Tory leader that relates to that. He may not be the kind of man you want to drink with or have at a party but he's still a good man.

AM: You could be a good person and not be a party person, and you could be a good person and be a party person but again all people are not the same. Like saying all Highlanders are the same or all MacDonalds are the same. That's like thinking of people as kind of clichés.

SR: The awfulness of over-simplification.

AM: The awfulness of over-simplification.

SR: Saying thank you for your short stories and the novel is an awful over-simplification. But I thank you and thank you for this conversation in your Cape Breton home.

AM: Thank you, thank you.

The Vision of Alistair MacLeod

JANE URQUHART

Each time I read the stories in *As Birds Bring Forth the Sun and Other Stories*, I am struck by the largeness of Alistair MacLeod's main characters. This is not only a largeness of physical stature but also, and more important, a largeness of soul, a generosity of spirit. Reflective and emotional without being self-conscious, his men are intimate, not just with women and children, but with the rough beauty of their geography, the old sorrows of their family legends, the sanctity of work, the mating cycles and slaughter of their animals: in short, with life itself. Although the presence of the "anima" in general is strong and benign in these stories, they are really about the masculine spirit, its strengths and its vulnerabilities. Time and again we are put in mind of the old Celtic heroes, of Oisin arguing ethics with Saint Patrick or of Finn McCool mourning the loss of his beloved dog Bran. And yes, at the same time, we are brought into closer contact with the men who are part of our own world and who are our friends and our family.

Like many other Canadians of Irish or Scottish background, MacLeod himself was brought up in the midst of a tribal, Celtic family much given to remembering the past and measuring the present in terms of it. In such families the tales of previous generations are told spontaneously and repetitively as a means of establishing both geographically and emotionally where the family has been, where it is now, and where it is going. In MacLeod's fiction the "voice" of the oral tradition is never far away and in some cases is as close as the opening sentences of a story. "Once there was a family with a Highland name who lived beside the sea," we are told in "As Birds Bring Forth the Sun." "And the man had a dog of which he was very fond." In the space of a few short sentences we, the readers, have joined the family, have entered the rooms of their houses, and have gathered together to hear the remainder of the tale. By the time the story is finished, the identification is so complete that we feel the hair rising on the backs of our own necks and hear the claws of the *cù mòr glas*, the big grey dog, scratching at our own doors. Moreover, a brilliant transformation has taken place. By skillfully interweaving past and present, recurring images and sensual detail, MacLeod creates a complex tapestry out of a seemingly simple and much-told family tale.

MacLeod's stories have been called – albeit with great admiration – traditional, even conservative, by a literary world cluttered with theories and "isms." They are, however, in their portrayal of an ancestral past that continually affects the present and in their sense of deep yearning for forsaken landscapes, as fresh and complex as the present moment. We Canadians are, after all, a nation composed of people longing for a variety of abandoned homelands and the tribes that inhabited them, whether these be the distant homelands of our recent immigrants, the abducted homelands of our natives peoples, the rural homelands vacated by the post-war migrations to the cities, or the various European or Asian homelands left behind by our earliest settlers. All of us have been touched in some way or another by this loss of landscape and of kin, and all of us are moved by the sometimes unidentifiable sorrow that accompanies such a loss. We are also moved, however, by the comfort we are afforded when an artist of the calibre of Alistair MacLeod carries such sorrowful and penetrating themes towards us in his gentle and capable hands.

These themes are not only Canadian ones, of course, they are universal – migration having always been a part of the human experience – and in MacLeod's stories, as in all great art, the universal becomes clearer and sharper when we are brought into intimate contact with the particular. I am always impressed, for instance, by the tension MacLeod creates in this country of vast distances and brutal weather by the anticipated journey home. A young man wishing to return to Cape Breton for Christmas from a job on Ontario lake freighters is dependent on the Great Lakes freezing, on the one hand, and on the highways being free of crippling blizzards on the other. A boy relies on a golden dog to guide him towards his warm kitchen and away from his death on a partly frozen sea. A crew of shaft and development miners knows that if one of them dies underground, as is so often the case, his comrades will make the dangerous winter journey to ferry the broken body back to the ancestral graveyard. A group of scattered relatives is aware that they will attempt to drive the long highways home to attend the funeral of a loved one despite the fear that the journey will be rendered impossible by winter, circumstance, change, or the fact that the return itself may be almost too painful to be borne. As the exiled narrator in "Winter Dog" laments:

> Should we be forced to drive tonight, it will be a long, tough journey into the wind and the driving snow which is pounding across Ontario and Quebec and New Brunswick and against the granite coast of Nova Scotia. Should we be drawn by death, we might well meet our own.

And in the middle of the long, multi-layered, and disturbing story entitled "Vision," the grandfather quotes the poem reputed to have been uttered thirteen hundred years ago by Saint Colum Cille upon his exile from Ireland:

> There is a grey eye
> Looking back on Ireland,
> That will never see again
> Her men or her women.
>
> Early and late my lamentation,
> Alas, the journey I am making;
> This will be my secret bye-name
> "Back turned on Ireland."

MacLeod's stories are resonant with the lamentations of exiles, and strong within these lamentations is the desire to preserve that which was, and even that which is, against the heartbreaking ravages of time; to preserve, not necessarily with factual accuracy, but rather with something that one can only call, trite though it sounds, emotional truth. Like the fishermen in "Vision" and in the interests of this goal, MacLeod defines his boundaries by making use of "the actual river" when it suits his purposes or, when it does not, "an earlier imaginary river which [he] can no longer see." Hence a tale from the past sheds as much clear light on a character or a situation as a contemporary word or deed and, in the end, preservation is accomplished by establishing the timelessness of legend.

To explore timelessness, preservation and emotional truth is among the purest of literary intentions and, because of this, the seven stories in *As Birds Bring Forth the Sun and Other Stories* seem to move effortlessly from the author's heart to the page and then to leap back from the page into the heart of the reader. This is not to suggest that there is anything resembling a "stream-of-consciousness" approach in the writing. In fact, MacLeod is so "care-full," in the true sense of the word, that quite the opposite is true. All of the stories have been "tuned to perfection" both technically and emotionally and with such care that they burst into sensual life as we read. We see and feel the cold, wet nose of the beloved dog, the delicate form of an embryo calf exposed within the slaughtered body of its mother, captured lobsters moving awkwardly on the floor of a fishing boat. But, most important, we are witness to a deepness of caring that binds man to woman, father to son, man to animal, and humanity to kin and landscape.

The depth of caring that is examined in *As Birds Bring Forth the Sun and Other Stories* is as much active as it is reflective in its expression. All the protagonists are men whose lives are inexorably bound to the physical: the netting of fish, the husbandry of animals, the carving of rock from the bowels of the earth. Almost immediately the reader comes to trust the heavy, muscular presence of such men who in many cases carry the history of their physicality around with them in the form of wounds or scars. Even the entry of a family story concerning old sorrows into the mind and memory of a young man is described actively, physically, and compared to wounds and scars. "You know," says the narrator in "Vision," "the future scar will be forever on the outside while the memory will remain, forever, deep within." By associating memory with blood and body, MacLeod suggests that emotion is biological and genetic and can never, therefore, be connected to that which is ephemeral or casual.

In the end it is this utter absence of the casual that gives MacLeod's stories their enormous power and raises them to the level of myth. "Second Spring" is much more than the tale of a Maritime boy "smitten with the calf club wish." It reaches back through time to all the sacred bulls and cows that have existed in Celtic, Greek, and Eastern myth. The *cù mòr glas*, which in the title story operates, for one family, as a sort of canine banshee, is equally Finn McCool's great dog Bran loping across the Giant's Causeway from Ireland to Scotland and Charon's dog Cerebus guarding the gates to the underworld and keeping watch over the River Styx. In "Vision" references to second sight, blindness, memory and a constant shifting of understanding call to mind the blindfolded figure of justice and cause us to examine the nature of perception itself.

One winter night I was fortunate enough to hear Alistair MacLeod read from new fiction. I took home that evening images of knives and forks being placed on a kitchen floor by children playing store, a nocturnal winter landscape viewed through glass, and, in the distance, one lantern going dark and another coming to rest far out on the ice. Like the old masters in W. H. Auden's "Musée des Beaux Arts," MacLeod is never wrong about suffering and understands "how it takes place/While someone else is eating or opening a window or just walking dully along;" or "how everything turns away/Quite leisurely from the disaster." But it is not the leisurely turning away that commands the focus of MacLeod's attention. Somewhere around the middle of the piece he read that night, he described a dog whose passion leads him to a tragedy as final as the one that visited his lantern-carrying owners. Someone, a grandfather I believe, says, "It was in those dogs to care too much, to try too hard," meaning that this exaggerated trying and caring was bred into such dogs in Scotland over 150 years ago. Sitting in the audience, I was suddenly convinced that MacLeod was describing not only a certain breed of dog but all his characters, animal and human, and the writer himself, engaged in his craft.

That is what we want from our best authors: not merely that they care and try but that they care *too* much and try *too* hard, that the intensification of feeling and of meaning manifest itself in their hearts and in their work. We come away from the stories in *As Birds Bring Forth the Sun and Other Stories* with that desire completely satisfied, our own world view intensified, enlarged, and enriched. And we come away understanding more clearly "the twisted strands within the rope," the difficult, "tangled twisted strands of love."

From Clan to Nation

ORALITY AND THE BOOK IN ALISTAIR MACLEOD'S *No Great Mischief*

DAVID WILLIAMS

One of the more intriguing features of Alistair MacLeod's first novel, *No Great Mischief*, is its re-staging of the Battle of the Plains of Abraham at a uranium mine on the Shield of Northern Ontario some two hundred years after the fact. A clan of Cape Breton Highlanders fights a drunken battle with a group of French-Canadian miners, ending in the death of Fern Picard, the Quebecois leader, and in the conviction for second-degree murder of Calum Mac-Donald, the narrator's brother and head of the Cape Breton miners. While the death of Picard gestures toward the death of General Montcalm, Calum's fate hardly resembles that of his ancestral clansmen who fell in the ranks of the 78th Highlanders at Quebec under the command of General James Wolfe. Nor does the novel ever refer to *The Death of General Wolfe*, that icon of imperial hagiography produced in 1771 by Benjamin West, a painter from the Thirteen Colonies (Warner 214). To the contrary, General Wolfe is portrayed throughout as a hidden foe of the Highlanders. As the narrator's maternal grandfather explains:

He was just using them against the French . . . Wolfe
referred to the Highlanders as his secret enemy and
once, speaking of recruiting them as soldiers in a letter to his friend Captain Rickson, he made the cynical
comment, "No great mischief if they fall" (108-09).
From the title page onward, the novel resists imperial
interpretations of the Conquest, suggesting that the
French and Scots, based on the logic of the implied
adage – my enemy's enemy must be my friend – are
likely unwitting allies.

More explicitly, the novel depicts the Cape Breton and
Quebecois as allies in loss, particularly in the overthrow
of their respective feudal societies at Culloden (1746) and
Quebec (1759). The standard of imperial glory, including
whatever shares of spoils fell to the Highlanders at Quebec in 1759, is raised by one MacDonald grandfather –
who boasts of "a French-speaking MacDonald who got
them past the sentries" – only to be dashed by another
MacDonald grandfather, who exposes a seam of vain-
glory in the myth:

> "They were first [up the cliff] because they were the
> best," said Grandpa stoutly. "I think of them as win-
> ning Canada for *us*. They learned that at Culloden."
> . . . "At Culloden they were on the *other* side," said
> Grandfather in near exasperation. "MacDonald fought
> *against* Wolfe. Then he went to Paris. That's where
> he learned his French. Then he was given a pardon
> so that he could fight *for* the British Army. He fought
> against Wolfe at Culloden and then fought for him
> years later at Quebec. Perhaps you can't blame Wolfe
> for being suspicious under the circumstances. He had
> a memory like other men. Still MacDonald died fight-
> ing *for* the British Army, not *against* it. And one

doesn't like to think of people giving their best, even their lives, under deceptive circumstances." (108)

The ultimate deception practiced by the British in the novel is evidently their subversion of the relationship of French and Celt, recalled in the ancestral Highlands by one old Scot to the narrator's sister, Catriona Macdonald Pankovich, who is on a visit from Canada: "The prince was here, you know . . . Bonnie Prince Charlie. Right at this very spot. He came from France in the summer of 1745 to fight for Scotland's crown. We were always close to France" (162). In the context of the Auld Alliance, the Conquest of Quebec takes on the character of a civil war, while the murder of Fern Picard by a descendant of the 78th Highlanders carries more than a hint of fratricide.

The narrator, Alexander MacDonald, is almost alone on this side of the Atlantic, however, in recognizing the "auld alliance" of French and Scots. While giving English lessons to a fellow miner from Quebec, he finds himself "pointing to *une chaîne, la dynamite, la poudre, la poudre de mine*, being impressed and surprised by how similar many of our words were although our accents were different. It seemed, at times, as if Marcel Gingras and I had been inhabitants of different rooms in the same large house for a long, long time" (199). Besides his sister Catriona, only Alexander's Grandma, the paternal grandmother who raised him, seems to share this understanding:

> When I used to read I used to think that they were a lot like us. That they were alone with their landscape for a long, long time. That it went into them somehow. Our friend used to say that long ago in

Scotland, they were our friends, part of the "auld alliance," they used to call it (269).

But the underground miners at Elliot Lake know only the
ancient division and fierce rivalries which still keep them
apart: "We viewed them, as they did us, with a certain
wariness; always on the lookout for the real or imagined
slight or advantage; being like rival hockey teams, wait-
ing for the right time to question stick measurements or
illegal equipment; biding our time and keeping our eyes
open" (171). Such behaviour, of course, is fundamentally
clannish: "Those are the Highlanders," [the others]
would say, "from Cape Breton. They stay mostly to themselves" (137). Yet Fern Picard's troop of miners appear to
observe the same rules as the Gaelic clan: "We never
entered their bunkhouses, as they never entered ours. It
would have been like going into the dressing room of the
opposing team" (147). In this war of the clans one sees
reflected the political problem of a nation. So the aesthetic
problem of the novel is how to formally integrate such
groups, divided by language and old blood feuds, into a
larger vision of the nation in this text written in English.
And where is the book that could cross a gulf so deep?

At one point only do the warring miners come to
acknowledge their kinship, when a James Bay Cree begins to play the fiddle. Then Quebecois and Highlander
alike "would join one another in the common fabric of
music. Gradually the titles from the different languages
seemed to fade away almost entirely, and the music was
largely unannounced or identified merely as *'la bastrin-
gue,'* 'an old hornpipe,' 'la guige,' 'a wedding reel,' *'un
reel sans nom'*" (154). Still, the aboriginal fiddler forms a
cultural bridge at the cost of his own cultural suppres-

sion. For, as a Métis of mixed blood and heritage, he is admitted to the company of Highlanders on the basis of the tribal shibboleth:

> *"Cousin agam fhein,"* he said in a mixture of English and Gaelic . . . He told us that his own name was James MacDonald and he had recognized the tartan on the shirt of the red-haired Alexander MacDonald, which I had been wearing at the time. The English/Gaelic phrase meant "cousin of my own" (151).

This phrase admits him to the *"clann Chalum Ruaidh"* (145), since he shared their blood and their language. But in ways that remain unspoken, his mixed heritage serves as a figure of the Highlanders' own alloyed language and cultural identity, since they too are neither one race nor the other, but both.

The Cape Breton *clann Chalum Ruaidh* are descended from Calum MacDonald, a Celtic survivor of the Battle of Culloden and Butcher Cumberland's bloody work of suppression which decimated the clan society of the Highlanders. "Anyone who knows the history of Scotland, particularly that of the Highlands and the Western Isles in the period around 1779, is not hard pressed to understand the reasons for their leaving" (20). But the Highland culture which the first *Calum Ruaidh* brings to the shores of Cape Breton can't maintain its privileged insularity in the New World. Perhaps an island fastness would hold the English language at bay for two or three generations. But once Grandpa and Grandma MacDonald become "dwellers of the town instead of dwellers of the country" (37), they "become quite adept at English" (40). For the language of the town is English, where Gaelic is the language of the country. Temporarily, reverse migration will produce an opposite effect: "In the time following their return to the old *Calum Ruadh* house and land, my brothers spoke Gaelic more and more, as if somehow by returning to the old land they had returned to the old language of that land as well. It being still the language of the place in which they worked" (64). And yet it is clear that Gaelic is threatened by urbanization. Although the grandparents are said to dream "almost totally in Gaelic" in their old age, "As if it had always been the language of their hearts," the narrator's sister finds her hope for the future in a book written in English: "There is a passage by Margaret Laurence in *The Diviners* where Morag talks about lost languages lurking inside the ventricles of the heart" (193). But if Gaelic is the sentimental language of the heart, English is still the working language of the book.

Herein lies a crucial tension in the novel between orality and literacy, the spoken and the written. "Primary orality," as Walter J. Ong argues, "fosters personality structures that in certain ways are more communal and externalized, and less introspective than those common among literates. Oral communication unites people in groups. Writing and reading are solitary activities that throw the psyche back on itself" (69). Although Gaelic speakers in the novel remain deeply embedded within their oral culture, that culture is also contained within the structures (and strictures) of print. So the aesthetic problem of the novel becomes a search for some means of integrating these communal structures of personality, marked by traits of orality, into the more individualistic and introspective structures of personality shaped by

writing. The narrator is at first unable, for example, to
recognize his own name when a roll call is taken in
English on his first day at school: "That's him, *gille beag
ruadh*, Alexander" (18), one of his cousins explains to a
teacher who doesn't understand the Gaelic phrase.
"Thankfully, however, we were of the generation who
were no longer beaten because we uttered Gaelic, 'beaten
for your own good,' as the phrase seemed to go, 'so you
will learn English and become good Canadian citizens.'
Instead she merely asked, 'Is your name Alexander?'"
(19). The distinction is vital, since names like Calum and
Alexander recall a long line of ancestors, thus reducing
the individual to a function of the group. Even worse, the
narrator must share "his" name with two cousins, one
local and one in California. With so much of his individu-
ality subsumed by the clan, each Alexander can only be
identified by his distinguishing marks. So, to his older
brother Calum, the narrator is "Still the *gille beag ruadh*,"
which means "the little red boy" or "the little red-haired
boy" (18).

Even Calum is reduced in long stretches of the narrative to "my eldest brother," identified by his relationship
with the speaker rather than by his "own" name. In
consequence, "my second brother" (177), like a third
brother, is not even named in this book of 283 pages; each
man simply acts and speaks as a part of his group.
Likewise, the absence of individual portraits of their dead
mother and father comes to symbolize personality structures which are communal and externalized: "There are
no pictures of our parents by themselves. They are always in large groups of *clann Chalum Ruaidh*" (240). Even
the attempt to "separate our parents" from their group

by means of a photographic enlargement is self-defeating in this context: "the individual features of their faces became more blurred. It was as if in coming closer they became more indistinct" (241). Here is graphic evidence of the claim that the individual has no identity apart from the clan.

"The clan," as one contemporary historian has written of pre-Culloden society, "remained a man's only identity, and the broadsword his only understandable law outside it" (Prebble 34). Vestiges of swordlaw still appear in Cape Breton, this place so distant from Culloden in time and space, though still recognizable in the *clann Chalum Ruaidh's* refusal to accept the authority of Canadian law, as well as in the inability of Canadians to recognize individuals apart from their group: "We've come for MacDonald," said the officer in charge. There was a ripple of laughter through the crowd and various shouts of 'Right here.' 'Over here.' All of the officers were from outside the local area and it probably had not entered their minds that almost all of us were named Mac-Donald" (125). At a wake for the dead cousin Alexander MacDonald, the Mounties most assuredly do not get their man; they are stymied by a social system depending on the rights and responsibilities of the clan, not of the individual. Citing an eighteenth-century clansmen to the effect that "It required no small degree of courage, and a greater degree of power than men are generally possessed of, to arrest an offender or debtor in the midst of his Clan" (35), Prebble outlines the basis of swordlaw as consisting of ties of blood, not in principles of jurisprudence or legal abstractions.

In reality, "The feudal framework which the power

of the chiefs gave to the Highland way of life enclosed a tribal system much older in time. The ties of blood and name were strong among the people, and pride of race meant as much to a humbly in his sod and roundstone house as it did to a chieftain in his island keep" (Prebble 33-34). Such ties of blood and name are what still bind the *clann Chalum Ruaidh* together. Both the narrator's grandparents, for example, have a great affection and respect for his maternal grandfather, partly out of recognition of their dependence on him: "He has always stood by us," said Grandma. "He has always been loyal to his blood. He has given us this chance" (35). Evidently, the duties and mores of the clan remain what they were in Scotland two centuries before, "each man owing economic allegiance to those above him, and all bound in fealty to the chieftain whose direct and known progenitor had been the strong-loined hero who had started the whole tribe" (Prebble 36). Early on, Grandfather MacDonald has ensured that his counterpart will have a career as caretaker at the hospital he himself has built in town.

Such a system of clan loyalties does not fit comfortably on everyone. As a child, the narrator would bridle at older people who demanded, "What's your name?" "What's your father's name?" "What's your mother's father's name?" And almost without fail, in the case of myself and my cousins, there would come a knowing look across the face of our questioners and they would say, in response to our answer, "Ah, you are the *clann Chalum Ruaidh,* as if that somehow explained everything" (28). But as young Alexander comes of age, clan loyalties do begin to explain everything, as the college student discovers the summer he is expected to give up his scholarship and take the place of his dead cousin in the mine: "My brother looked at me and I, in turn, looked at the faces of my grandparents and at the parents of the red-haired Alexander MacDonald. I nodded my head slightly" (131). Just as the clansmen at Culloden "came out when told, most of them, pulling broadswords from the sod where they had been hidden since the Disarming Acts that followed the last rebellion" (Prebble 51), so the *gille beag ruadh* takes his cousin's place with his older brothers in their feud with Fern Picard.

Not surprisingly, the Gallic clan comes to resemble its Gaelic counterpart in everything but language. Super-ficially, their system of economic and social obligations is almost the same: "We heard also that Fern Picard had approached Renco Development the day following Alex-ander MacDonald's death with the proposition that he could bring in another crew of his own relatives from Temiskaming to replace *clann Chalum Ruaidh* in the shaft's bottom" (171). More profoundly still, the whole culture of Quebecois and Highlander is based on an economy of memory. When Calum encounters a group of Picard's men on a Toronto street after his release from prison, he intuits as much, even if he can't explain it: "I recognized their license plates, *Je me souviens*, at about the same time I noticed their driving" (187). His selection of this significant detail merges with one of this own typical locutions to explain what he glimpses in the other culture: "We have come a long way, you and I, and there are no hard feelings," he says to the narrator early in the novel. "Do you remember Christy?" (11).

"Do you remember" is a phrase which begins to reverberate throughout the whole of the narrative. "Do you remember," [the narrator's sister] asked, "when Grandpa would drink his whiskey and how he would start to cry when he told the story about the dog going back across the ice to the island?" (95). Again, "Remember," asked my sister, "how Grandpa and Grandma used to dream?" (193). "Do you remember the well, *'ille bhig ruaidh?*" his brothers ask him while reminiscing at the mine one afternoon (174). And so the catechism goes: "Remember when we lived in the old house and we would go outside right before going to bed to check the weather for the next day? . . . Do you remember?" "Yes, I remember" (186). The catechetical phrase echoes the formula of memory in oral societies with their bounden duty to preserve the past in repetitive speech, since, without written texts, their very history would soon vanish.

Even in the greeting of Marcel Gingras to this man who has killed his own leader, there sounds an echo of the *clann Chalum Ruaidh* formula: "This is *Calum Mor*," he said. "Long time ago when we first came with Fern Picard, this was the best miner we ever saw" (188). *We have come a long way, you and I, and there are no hard feelings. Do you remember the old days at Elliot Lake?* In oral culture, as Ong describes it, memory has to be "agonistically toned": "By keeping knowledge embedded in the human lifeworld, orality situates knowledge within a context of struggle" (Ong 43). So the fatal struggle between the miners in this novel is transformed into a source of knowledge, later becoming a point of pride for other miners. *This was the best miner we ever saw.*

The affirmation, *I remember,* like the catechism, *Do you remember?*, is not the only formula of memory in the

novel. A whole body of songs preserves the memories
and dreams of each group: "Sometimes Marcel Gingras
would sing one or two songs to us, although they often
surpassed our understanding. They affected him,
though, quite deeply and sometimes his eyes would fill
with embarrassed mist as he ran his hand over the tat-
tered map, outlining the lines that did not visually exist.
They existed, however, for him, and in the old dream: *le
pays des Laurentides*" (248). This Laurentian country,
straddling the border of two provinces, harkens back to
a time before the region was partitioned by Confedera-
tion and apportioned to the new provinces of Quebec and
Ontario. Like Marcel, the narrator senses how "the people of that region had more in common with one another
than they had with those whom they felt controlled their
destinies form [sic] the distant cities of Toronto and Quebec City" (247) What is evidently recalled in Marcel's
songs is the ghostly presence of a lost homeland. In much
the same way, "the older singers or storytellers of the
clann Chalum Ruaidh, the *seanaichies*, as they were called
. . . would 'remember' events from a Scotland which they
had never seen" (65). For the lost Highland home, like *le
pays des Laurentides*, endures as a verbal presence that
cannot be lost so long as it still echoes in song.

But lost homelands can also be conjured up in less
spectral ways in the novel. When Catherine, the narrator's sister, visits Scotland, she is immediately recognized
by "strangers" in Moidart after an "absence" of two
centuries:

"You are from here," said the woman.
"No," said my sister, "I'm from Canada."
"That may be," said the woman. "But you are really

from here. You have just been away for a while."
(160)

At first, Catherine is incredulous at what she finds in
Moidart: "Some of them . . . had red hair and some had
hair as black or blacker than my own. All of them had the
same eyes. It was like being in Grandpa and Grandma's
kitchen" (163). Even more surprising than what she sees
is what she hears. For the Moidart MacDonalds have not
forgotten the beginning of her family's history, the story
of the loyal dog who, in its desperation not to be left
behind, swam out to the departing ship:

> "Yes," said the old man, nodding in the direction of
> the brown and white dogs, which lay like rugs be-
> neath the table and the chairs in the stone house in
> Moidart. "It was in those dogs to care too much and
> to try too hard" (166).

Word for word, it is the same phrase Grandpa MacDonald has used to describe the descendant of the original
dog who gave her life defending the lighthouse after the
death of the children's parents: "It was *in* those dogs to
care too much and to try too hard" (57). As it happens,
saying and doing carry a common pedigree, as if there
could be a bloodline and a voiceline reaching back to
Moidart in the Scottish Highlands, almost as if words, like
organic cells, could replicate their own DNA.

Once the story is picked up like a dropped stitch, the
lost homeland is indeed found again. And yet nothing
can change the reality of the Highland clearances, or the
necessity of economic migration from Cape Breton. In
fact, of all those "going down the road" from Cape

Breton, Catherine has gone the farthest away to drama
school in Alberta and a marriage in Calgary. So, too,
Alexander goes down the road to university in Halifax,
and on to a dental practice in Ontario, though he carries
with him a family history of dispossession and sorrow.
For his maternal grandfather has told him the painful
story of a man "crying for his history" (25), the first Calum
MacDonald to be set ashore in Nova Scotia's Pictou
County. On the day when Alexander graduates from
college, his other Grandpa protests against such ancient
tales of woe: "No more sad stories . . . Let's sing some
songs" (115). But as they celebrate in a car bound for Cape
Breton, the very song they choose to sing is *Cumha Ceap
Breatuinn*," the "Lament for Cape Breton." Somehow,
even the moment of homecoming turns into a ritual
lament. It is as if the word *home* is synonymous with the
memory of loss.

There is nonetheless good reason in oral culture for
such joy to be expressed in the form of sorrow. As Ong
explains, "oral societies must invest great energy in saying over and over again what has been learned arduously
over the ages. This need establishes a highly traditionalist
or conservative set of mind that with good reason inhibits
intellectual experimentation" (41). Prebble makes the
point that "the past lingered" on in Highland culture
"behind its defence-work of the Irish tongue, the memories kept alive by pipes and the songs" (34). So in a sense,
the keynote of the culture is formally determined. For
where "Song is the remembrance of songs sung" (Ong
146), then the context of the form must continue to be the
memory of other songs.

Whatever its own tonality, the "Lament for Cape

Breton" turns out to be the singers' joyful expression of
continuity with the past. For the memory of one song
recalls the memory of another, through the whole reper-
toire of *"Fail-ill-o Agus Ho Ro Eile," "Mo Nighean Dubh,"*
"O Chruinneag," "An T'altan Dubh," "Mo Run Geal Dileas,"
and *"O Siud An Taobh A Ghabhainn."* "We sang all the old
songs, the songs that people working together used to
sing to make a heavy task lighter. And as we drove by
the houses of 'our own country,' Grandpa would identify
or shout to his relatives as they stood beside their doors
or walked about their yards" (117). Ultimately, it is the
sound of Gaelic which is the reassuring sound of home,
"'God's country,' or 'our own country,' as he called it"
(116). And this country is virtually omnipresent in the
memory of the Gaelic songs which are sung. In that sense,
it really is not far off from *le pays des Laurentides de Marcel
Gingras.*

Lost homelands are not the only thing, however, that
the *clann Chalum Ruaidh* must recall. The children have
lost both their parents, one sibling, and an island home
on a single winter night when Mother, Father, and little
brother Colin are swept under the ice on their way home
to their lighthouse-keep. The oldest boy, sixteen-year old
Calum, and his two teen-age brothers, now retreat to the
farmhouse which their grandparents had once exchanged for town; and the twins, three-year-old Alexander and Catherine, are left in the care of the old ones.
"There are a lot of things I don't know," said Grandma,
"but there are some things I really believe in. I believe you
should always look after your blood. If I did not believe
that," she would say, "Where would you two be?" (58).

Evidently Grandma's way of knowing is traditional,

based on the maxims and proverbs of oral tradition. She "believed with great dedication in a series of maxims. 'Waste not, want not' was one, and 'Always look after your blood' was another" (38). Such formulae, as Ong has claimed, "help implement rhythmic discourse and also act as mnemonic aids in their own right, as set expressions circulating through the mouths and ears of all" (35). For the proverb, like the oral formula, works to subtend and extend the mutual obligations of the group. "My hope is constant in thee, Clan Donald," Grandpa says to Alexander's Grandfather, "which is what Robert the Bruce was supposed to have said to the MacDonalds at the Battle of Bannockburn in 1314" (88). "My hope is constant in thee, Clan Donald" (202), Grandpa repeats the maxim to Alexander over the long-distance wire, confirming the latter's obligation to pick up his San Francisco cousin in Sudbury. "Blood is thicker than water, as you've often heard us say" (203), Grandma enjoins the boy during the same telephone call. "My hope is constant in thee, Clan Donald" (191), Calum later says to the narrator, as Alexander takes leave of his wreck of a brother in his tenement apartment in Toronto. The truth is, the narrator feels the pull of Grandma's maxim as much as he feels the pull of kinship; if blood is thicker than water, then the sound of her voice must be thicker than printer's ink.

The values of sound in the novel nonetheless have to be expressed in the fixities of print. One of the paradoxes of the book is that print can still be used to communicate an oral feel for existence. As Ong maintains, "the phenomenology of sound enters deeply into human beings' feel for existence," although such a phenomenology typically appears in song and formulaic utterances of oral poetry. Since "writing restructures consciousness" (Ong 78), then the novelist who wishes to re-present this "oral" feel for existence must find unusual means. One of MacLeod's strategies is to reproduce a number of oral-aural settings from the lifeworld of the culture: "Sometimes, said my brothers, the blackfish [whales] would follow their boat, and they loved applause and appreciated singing . . . Sometimes when they were invisible my brothers would sing songs to them in either English or Gaelic" (99). This sense of continuity with the natural world recurs in many songs sung to other animals: "Even Christy was afraid as the high surf broke about her knees and her hooves slipped on the wet rocks she could not see. Calum grasped the cheek straps of her bridle in both his hands and we could hear him singing in Gaelic, loudly and clearly at the side of her head, in an attempt to steady and calm her, much as a parent might sing to a frightened child" (101). Music does soothe the savage beast, but only where it has civilized the "savage" beast. And song is not even the best marker of civility in the oral world.

"[O]ral memory," as Ong observes, "differs significantly from textual memory in that oral memory has a high somatic component" (67). In this novel, the ache of memory becomes so strong, it produces a pain that must find physical release.

> "Four years ago we were in Timmins," Calum continued, "and we talked all one day and night about the island. In the end, we couldn't stand it any longer so we phoned up Grandfather and first we asked him about the weather" (210-11).

In the end, not even speech will suffice to relieve their pain. So these hardrock miners pick up their tools and drive the fifteen hundred miles to the island where their parents died, to drill their initials "into the face of the rock. We drilled their initials and their dates and Colin's, too" (213). And when Grandpa MacDonald offer them some beer, hoping "It will help you to forget," their Grandfather MacDonald says quietly, "They didn't come all this way . . . because they wanted to forget" (215). The body, in fact, cannot forget. For such reasons, its feel for existence can be dominant, even when it is confined to print.

Another strategy for capturing an oral culture's feel for existence is in the mode of information, in the means by which the storyteller gains his knowledge: "Others told stories of forerunners; of how they had seen 'lights' out on the ice 'at the exact spot' years before, and of how such harbingers could now be seen as prophesies fulfilled" (54). Long stretches of the written narrative derive from such locutions: "One summer, my oldest brother told me, *clann Chalum Ruaidh* worked at Keno Hill in the Yukon" (141); "Once, my brother told me, they were working in the Bridge River Valley of British Columbia" (205); "'You won't remember any of this, *'ille bhig ruaidh*,' said my oldest brother. 'At that time you and your sister were only infants, sleeping in baskets by the stove'" (181). Apparently, the bulk of the story the narrator has to tell has been filtered through such mechanisms of oral culture: "This is a story of lives which turned out differently than was intended. And obviously much of this information is not really mine at all – not in the sense that I experienced it" (57). In such fashion, the narrator takes the place of one of the *seanaichies* who "'remember' events from a Scotland which they have never seen" (65).

All the same, it may be surprising to find a novel published in 1999 in a highly literate society masquerading in the voice of an oral speaker, as if it did not have its own being in print: "As I begin to tell this, it is the golden month of September in southwestern Ontario" (1). Even more disconcerting is the auditory role imagined for readers in the narrative: "The 401, as most people hearing this will know, is Ontario's major highway" (3). And so it goes: "The *Calum Ruadh* who seems so present in thought and conversation in today's Toronto was, as I mentioned earlier, my great-great-great-grandfather" (19-20). It is as if, by insisting on an oral relationship with the reader, the writer wishes to obviate his medium of communication. Yet this is not an age in which we are content to let media speak for themselves; the medium is the message, as we have been hearing since the early 1960s. If there is one true hallmark of postmodern culture, it is our awareness of painting as *painting*, and of writing as *writing*. Is it really possible, then, to ignore the form and skip directly to the content of art, or to pretend that a fiction is not really a fiction?

Admittedly, "Readers whose norms and expectations for formal discourse are governed by a residually oral mindset relate to a text quite different from readers whose sense of style is radically textual. The nineteenth-century novellist's [sic] nervous apostrophes to the 'dear reader'. . . suggest that the typical reader was felt by the writer to be closer to the old-style listener than most readers commonly are felt to be today" (Ong 171). The reason is that, "Well after printing was developed, auditory processing continued for some time to dominate the visible, printed text"(Ong 120). Just as significantly, "Manuscript culture in the west remained always marginally oral"(Ong 119). Cape Breton culture has itself remained residually oral, as its relative lack of printed fiction and its plethora of Gaelic music would suggest. So it may well be that a professor and writer at the University of Windsor would feel the need to invoke a "dear reader" formula. Or it may even be that a novel about an oral culture would inevitably be "marginally oral." But the fact remains that, in late twentieth-century culture, the book has become "less like an utterance, and more like a thing"(Ong 125).

The thing-ness of the book is what, at first blush, appears to be missing from *No Great Mischief.* The writer never seems to notice his page before him as he "speaks"; his words never seem to take their shape from ink of pen or typewriter ribbon, much less of a laser printer. And the only real concession he makes to questions of epistemology – of how he knows what he knows – is the familiar apologia borrowed from oral culture: "whatever its inaccuracies, this information has come to be known in the manner that family members come to know one another because they share such close proximity" (58).

Nor is it surprising that the plot is structured in the manner of oral narrative. For two thirds of the novel, the moment of narration is a frame into whose action the past washes up periodically: the narrator drives from Windsor to Toronto to tend to his derelict brother Calum; he hears him singing the "Lament for Cape Breton" as he goes out to the beer store, though, on his way, he is "almost surprised to realize [the song] is no longer com-

ing from him but from somewhere deep within me" (16).
Even when the well of memory begins to flow, the history
of the clan comes out in fits and starts which have more
to do with the structure of oral memory than with any
written history or chronology.

What the narrator does recall is most often determined by dramatic audiences who initiate, or continue,
or supplement the narrator's own act of remembrance.
So, for example, in his recollections of childhood, Alexander remembers his MacDonald grandfather recalling
the story of the first Calum Ruadh, "crying for his history" (25). Or again, Grandfather recalls the Battle of
Killiecrankie to Grandpa MacDonald while doing his
taxes (90 ff). But as soon as the tax return is filled out, the
Battle of Killiecrankie ended, the narrative leaps in the
ensuing chapter to Alexander at his sister's house in
Calgary, listening to Catherine tell of the murder of the
bard "Mac Ian" by his English guests. At the same time,
we are told of Grandpa MacDonald's tears on any occasion "he told the story about the dog going back across
the ice to the island" and "how he let her go because she
broke his heart" (95). Likewise following the story of
James MacDonald, the fiddler from James Bay, we are
returned to Catherine's house where she tells her story of
being taken for a native of Moidart, and of hearing the
tale from clansmen, two centuries removed from the
event, of the loyal MacDonald dog swimming after the
boat.

While such stories may be paired on a thematic level
(the return of the "native" in the instances of the James
Bay and Moidart MacDonalds), on the narrative level
they are more often triggered by associative memory. The

artistic skill by which these episodes are brought together is really more typical of oral narrative than of the book. As Ong notes, "What made a good epic poet was, among other things of course, first, tacit acceptance of the fact that episodic structure was the only way and the totally natural way of imagining and handling lengthy narrative, and, second, possession of supreme skill in managing flashback and other episodic techniques" (144). The novelist may exhibit the virtuosity of an oral poet in managing such shifts of time and place. This does not change the fact that an oral narrative strains at the seams of the printed book.

Take the frame narration of the narrator's trip to the liquor store which is recounted at intervals through portions of eight chapters (1, 8, 10, 12, 15, 16, 24, 27) extending from page 15 to page 185. If we are to read the frame narration as the imitation of an action, the action is about as credible as the wanderings of Odysseus; it could appear in the *Guinness Book of Records* as the longest trip in literature to the beer store. Like the wanderings of Odysseus, it is likewise filled with digressions which are oral memories of other sojourns: the narrator's journey to an orthodontists' conference in Dallas where he is asked, "Who are these Ukrainians one is always hearing about in Canada?" (59); to Toronto where he keeps remembering migrant workers along the highway, imagining them "imagining themselves back home" (71). Or else he produces a catalogue of what he hears and sees in "the canyons of Toronto streets . . . the voices of the protestors, the chants and songs and slogans of their beliefs, and the equally strong voices of those opposed to them. 'No cruise here,' they say. 'A strong defence is not an offence.'

'Say no to nuclear war'" (98). In some respects, these lists are much less typical of written narrative than they are of the catalogue of ships in Homer's *Illiad*, "where the names of persons and places occur as involved in doings" (Ong 42-3). In other words, the logic of the frame narration is "situational rather than abstract" (Ong 49), much in the manner of oral storytelling.

As it happens, the narrator's visit to his alcoholic brother in Toronto is not the whole of the frame narration. While the final chapter (43) preserves the fiction of a narrative (speaking) present, the scene has already shifted two full seasons ahead: "And now it is six months later and the phone rings" (276). The month is March, the same month as the parents fell through the ice all those years ago, and Calum is on the other end of the line, saying, "It's time." Arbitrarily time for another journey, this time by car. So Alexander will drive from Windsor to Toronto, pick up Calum and head east into Quebec: "At Rivière du Loup we turn south towards New Brunswick" (278). In fact, the rest of the route is carefully charted: Grand Falls, Plaster Rock, Renous, Rogersville, Moncton, Sackville, Antigonish, Havre Boucher Hill. And so they arrive in sight of the island lighthouse off the coast of Cape Breton where their parents died so many years ago. And where, at peace in the passenger seat beside his watchful brother, Calum now dies as well. At which point the narrator thinks, "This is the man who carried me on his shoulders when I was three. Carried me across the ice from the island, but could never carry me back again." In a sense, the narrator is nonetheless able to carry his brother back again: "Ferry the dead. *Fois do t'anam*. Peace to his soul" (283). For the frame narrative is really more than a vehicle for oral memory; it has been this vehicle, all along, to ferry the dead to the ancestors.

In other respects, the frame narration is much different in kind from the oral narrative of the clan. For one thing, it has no auditors, meaning that the story is less "the result of interaction between the singer, the present audience, and the singer's memories of songs sung" (Ong 146). Nor, in most of these framing chapters, is there much conversation, since the action is dominated by the solitary consciousness of the narrator. Here, the quotation marks of speech, which are typical of the ongoing conversation carried on in the scenes of oral history, get inverted, and are turned inward.

The style of the frame narration also differs from the oral style, going beyond the usual somatic triggers of memory to a philosophic form of questioning. Many of its sentences shift from a situational to an abstract logic: "The children [of the migrant pickers] will grasp their parents' browned hands. They will be asked to take a number and later to answer the complicated question of exactly who they are . . . All of [the migrant workers from Quebec] will point out to their children the superiority of Quebec's highway rest areas compared to those of Ontario, indicating the plenitude of free hot water and the lack of commercial pressures. They will rest easily within the boundaries of their region" (197). In the end, what we hear in such passages is the inwardness and reflectiveness of a mind structured by writing.

Likewise in the end, the effects of writing on the narrator's consciousness have an unforeseen political consequence. For what he notes on the borders of his family history, and what he writes in the margins of their oral memories, adds up to a vision of the nation. From the imagined inclusion of Ukrainians in Canada to the nameless workers invited by signs in the fields along the highways "to 'pick your own' and whole families can be seen doing exactly that" (1), the narrator is engaged in cataloguing the plurality of the nation, from oilmen (and his sister married to a Slav) in Calgary, to ethnic miners (and his own brothers) in Northern Ontario, to Celtic fishermen (and his remaining family) in Nova Scotia. And always in their midst are other families, these migrants who, like the folk from Cape Breton, are "going down the road": "They do not 'pick your own' but pick instead for wages to take with them when they leave. This land is not their own. Many of them are from the Caribbean and some are Mennonites from Mexico and some are French Canadians from New Brunswick and Quebec" (1). But, whatever their economic or immigrant status, they are all imagined as potential fellow citizens. In that respect, at least, the book is a virtual instrument of citizenship.

While there may be some truth to Marshall McLuhan's claim that "The tribe, an extended form of a family of blood relatives, is exploded by print, and is replaced by an association of men homogeneously trained to be individuals" (*Understanding* 161), MacLeod's novel suggests that the tribe can persist in the structures of writing, even on the point of assimilation into the "nation" of the book. By contrast, McLuhan's sense of this shift from tribe to nation is more absolute, and mostly ahistorical: "Only the phonetic alphabet makes a break between eye and ear, between semantic meaning and visual code; and thus only phonetic writing has the power to translate man from the tribal to the civilized sphere, to give him an eye for an ear" (*Gutenberg* 27). In effect, this is to make an unwarranted leap of logic from the cognitive to political effects of alphabetic writing.

A better historical explanation for the part played by the book in the formation of nations is offered by Benedict Anderson. He maintains that the novel and the newspaper have fundamentally changed our sense of time and space. For a new sense of simultaneous experience becomes available to readers who now share the same stories, as well as the same rituals of reading, both of which are "performed in silent privacy, in the lair of the skull." In the case of the newspaper, "this ceremony is incessantly repeated at daily of half-daily intervals through the calendar. What more vivid figure for the secular, historically clocked imagined community can be envisioned?" (Anderson 35). As for ways in which the novel has changed our perceptions of space, Anderson sees "the 'national imagination' at work in the movement of a solitary hero through a sociological landscape of a fixity that fuses the world inside the novel with the world outside. This picaresque *tour d'horizon* –hospitals, prisons, remote villagers, monasteries, Indians, Negroes – is nonetheless not a *tour de monde*. The horizon is clearly bounded" (Anderson 30).

The horizon of *No Great Mischief* is most clearly bounded by the geography (not to mention the ethnography) of the nation, not just the clan. For the landscape through which Calum is ferried on his final journey to his ancestors is envisioned from the first page of the novel as a large-scale project of mapping: "Along Highway 3 the roadside stands are burdened down by baskets of produce and arrangements of plants and flowers" (1); "In the fall and in the spring I take the longer but more scenic routes: Highway 2 and Highway 3 and even sometimes Highways 98 or 21" (2); "The 401 . . . is Ontario's major highway and it runs straight and true from the country that is the United States to the border of Quebec, which some might also consider another country" (3). Not surprisingly, this mapping consciousness is present in scenes of oral memory, and is still preoccupied with charting the larger territory: "We started out driving westward [from Sudbury] on Highway 17, past Whitefish, and McKerrow, and the road to Espanola. Past Webbwood and Massey and Spanish and Serpent River" (132); "We went outside the house [in Calgary] and looked down from the prestigious ridge. It was late afternoon and in the distance we could see the cars streaming east along the Trans-Canada Highway. Coming from Banff and the B.C. border" (167). In such fashion, the vehicle of the book carries us out of the territory of clan and into the geography of the nation.

In another sense as well, the shift from clan to nation is a shift from the resources of an oral culture to the new and more spacious possibilities of the book. For the narrator, who retains many oral values, is also a bilingual citizen of print, as others are quick to point out. In reporting the story of meeting Marcel Gingras in a car with plates bearing the motto "Je me souviens," Calum tells his brother that Marcel "asked about you – 'the book one,' they used to call you" (189). Alexander is clearly more comfortable in the library than in the mines, happy to send his grandfather to the college library to confirm the telltale phrase of Wolfe that it would be "No great mischief if they fall" (109).

In the very differences between the grandfathers are likewise encoded many of the fundamental tensions of the narrative. Where Grandfather MacDonald is soberly reflective, introspective and private, in the manner of the literate man, Grandpa MacDonald is cheerfully spontaneous, impulsive, and sociable, in the fashion of the oral man. "Grandpa died from jumping up in the air and trying to click his heels together twice . . . When he died, Grandfather said, 'What an absolutely foolish way for a man to die.'" On the other hand, "Grandfather died reading a book called *A History of the Scottish Highlands*" (264). In the persons of these two men, the many tensions in the narrator's character are finally resolved. For what he really manages to do in writing this oral story is to reconcile opposed ways of knowing in a style which is true to each.

Ultimately, what Alistair MacLeod has achieved in his novel is more than a "song" of remembered songs, or even an oral memory of lost homelands. In the largest sense, it is a print creation of the imagined nation, of that dreamed home in the book where Highlander and Quebecois may truly live in harmony with Ukrainians, Mennonites, and migrant workers from Mexico. It could nearly pass for a long-lost map of the peaceable kingdom.

WORKS CITED

Anderson, Benedict. *Imagined Communities: Reflections on the Origin and Spread of Nationalism*. 1983. rev.ed. London & New York: Verso, 1991.

MacLeod, Alistair. *No Great Mischief*. Toronto: McClelland & Stewart, 1999.

McLuhan, Marshall. *The Gutenberg Galaxy: The Making of Typographic Man*. Toronto: UTorontoP, 1962.

Understanding Media: The Extensions of Man. 1964. 2nd. ed. Toronto: Signet, 1966.

Ong, Walter J. *Orality and Literacy: The Technologizing of the Word*. London & New York: Methuen, 1982.

Prebble, John. *Culloden*. 1961. Harmondsworth, Middlesex: Penguin, 1967.

Warner, Oliver. *With Wolfe to Quebec: The Path to Glory*. Toronto: Collins, 1972.

Loved Labour Lost

ALISTAIR MACLEOD'S
ELEGIAC ETHOS

JANICE KULYK KEEFER

Perhaps there is no finer, more succinct expression of the defining features of Alistair MacLeod's fiction than Jane Urquhart's "The Vision of Alistair MacLeod," an essay printed in the present volume. "Largeness of soul, generosity of spirit" are attributes, Urquhart suggests, not only of MacLeod's characters, but of the writer himself. What we most cherish in MacLeod's work, she goes on to say, is that "intensification of feeling and of meaning" achieved by fiction which explores, through sensuously detailed particulars, the human need for "timelessness . . . and emotional truth." Urquhart is just as accurate in pinpointing MacLeod's principal theme or obsession as "the lamentations of exiles," a theme she finds to be a constant in human experience, especially in Canada. Yet "strong within these lamentations" she finds "the desire to preserve that which was" in ways which will resonate to the most contemporary of readers scanning MacLeod's imagined communities and cultural geography for some outline of the future.

What I wish to draw attention to in this essay, however, is not any element of timelessness and universality in MacLeod's tropes and plots, inscribed as they are by his Celtic heritage, but rather the rootedness of his fiction in the historical as well as cultural specifics of Cape Breton. The historical, in MacLeod's work, encompasses Culloden and the Highland clearances, of course – and now, in *No Great Mischief*, the Highland key to the winning of the Battle of the Plains of Abraham. But it also includes a sharp awareness of labour history, the narrative of those whose lives and possibilities have been determined as much by the price of fish and coal, and the pay packets of those who produce these commodities, as by the songs and stories of their displaced Highland ancestors. In MacLeod's writing, labour and lyrical are intertwined, not antithetical: his celebration and lamentation for the disappearance of the traditional forms of masculine labour indigenous to Nova Scotia prove to be the apotheosis of his elegiac vision, as we find in his long-awaited novel, *No Great Mischief*.

For MacLeod's novel is no new departure but a consolidation and interweaving of tropes and subjects to be found in his earliest collection, *The Lost Salt Gift of Blood*. The theme on which I wish to focus in this paper is central to "The Boat," the story for which, up to now, he has been best known. That theme – the profound dignity and heroism of traditional forms of human labour, especially the difficult, risky and subsistence labour of fishing and mining – is especially prominent in *No Great Mischief*, from its very first pages to its last. And just as, in "The Boat," the main source of tension and conflict arises from the opposing choices made by father and son as to their life's work – fishing and teaching/writing – so too in *No Great Mischief*. In fact, the conflict is curiously reconfigured. First, the occupations of the two brothers, Calum and Alexander – miner and orthodontist – emerge as diametrically opposed, whereas the borders between fishing and the literary life in "The Boat" are fringed and permeable, with the fisherman-father in that story being a compulsive reader whose embrace of the punishing ways of the sea is as forced as any shotgun wedding. Second, the element of that Isaiah Berlin-like "tragic choice" which lends so much pathos to "The Boat" is entirely missing. For whereas the narrator of the story has rejected the fisherman's life so prized by his mother, he has chosen the differently difficult and lonely life of literature which forms the focus of his father's values. The narrator of *Mischief* is not forced into the position of having to make a choice between two equal, but incompatible goods; in fact, he himself underscores the fraudulence of his chosen profession. Throughout the novel, MacLeod insists upon the superficiality, triviality and even dishonesty of Alexander's life as defined by the so-called work he does; it possesses none of the value and usefulness of the time-honoured ways out of poverty: teaching and medicine, and it is damned by the value system upheld by Alexander's admirable grandmother, who judges orthodontistry to be man's attempt to improve on God's work, an attempt not so much impious as ridiculous.

The more MacLeod's novel foregrounds the uselessness and opportunism of a safe, respectable, remunerative profession that caters to people's vanity and plunders their wallets, the more it exalts the kind of skilled, laborious and largely thankless work which involves dirtying or cracking the hands, and risking life and limb. Given that MacLeod's vision of human life and possibility is insistently tragic – as Urquhart states, it is in MacLeod's cherished characters as well as their dogs to care too much and try too hard –Calum's personal tragedy emerges as both inevitable and in tune with the truth of things. That his work and ethos lead him to "ruin" his life by killing a fellow miner in a fight, serving a jail sentence, and taking to the bottle in a series of squalid rooming houses in the exile of Toronto – these factors do not disqualify him from, but rather, fit him for the kind of hero's return and funeral rites towards which the novel inexorably moves. What becomes increasingly clear to the reader is that shame is not the portion of the alcoholic brother, but rather the permanent burden of the up-wardly-mobile dentist in his pristine, respectable south-ern-Ontario suburb. It is a shame mixed with the guilt Alexander feels at the death, in a mining accident, of his cousin Alexander MacDonald, who had gone into the mine after high school "to help the members of his family who had been haunted, through no fault of their own, by the echoes of a kind of regional, generational poverty" (*NGM* 172-3). It is "the feeling of the callouses on [his cousin's] small, determined, hard-working hands" that is "permanently bonded" to Alexander's very sense of himself –Alexander, whose own hands, however skilled they may be in the intricacies of orthodontistry, can never be similarly hard-working (*NGM* 173). For they are tainted by what he calls "the pollution of prosperity" (*NGM* 192), a prosperity which also seems to afflict the affluent life of Alexander's melancholic twin sister.

Although the narrator of *No Great Mischief* does choose to forego a cushy summer scholarship to spend an extended period with his brothers and compatriots in a northern Ontario mining camp, this labour is really a swan song to the values and way of life of Cape Breton, the payment of a near-genetic debt before saying good-bye to all that. Life and labour in the camp run by Renco Development – a multinational mining company – is a far cry from the work ethic and aesthetic celebrated in "The Closing Down of Summer," the opening story of *As Birds Bring Forth the Sun*. In both works, we find, subtly deline-ated, the pressure of economics and industrial decline: the collapse of coal mining in the Maritimes has led to the displacement of Cape Bretoners. True, this is a very dif-ferent kind of exile from that suffered by those whose poverty forced them into factories and domestic service in New England. It is not their losses, but rather their skill and strength that take MacLeod's characters to the mines of South Africa and South America. But the narrator of "The Closing Down of Summer" is a man "from a mining family that has given itself for generations to the dark-ened earth" (*BBF* 29), and he is proud to carry on this tradition even if his children have abandoned it to follow law or dentistry, "mov[ing] their fat, pudgy fingers over the limited possibilities to be found in other people's mouths" (*BBF* 27):

I have always wished that my children could see me at my work . . .[;] see how articulate we are in the accomplishment of what we do. That they might ap-preciate the perfection of our drilling and the calcu-lation of our angles and the measuring of our powder, and that they might understand that what we know through eye and ear and touch is of a finer quality than any information garnered by the most

sophisticated of mining engineers with all their
elaborate equipment . . . I would like to show them
how . . . there is perhaps a certain eloquent beauty
to be found in what we do . . . the beauty of motion
on the edge of violence, which by its very nature
cannot very long endure . . . We are big men engaged
in perhaps the most violent of all occupations and we
have chosen as our adversary walls and faces of massive stone . . . In the chill and damp we have given
ourselves to the breaking down of walls and barriers.
We have sentenced ourselves to enclosures so that we
might taste the giddy joy of breaking through. Always hopeful of breaking through though we know
we will never break free. (*BBF* 28-30)

"Articulate" and "eloquent": these are the adjectives
used to convey the distinguishing characteristic of this
form of labour, so often associated with illiteracy and
ignorance. The miners are artists – writers, creating
beauty and the possibility of that kind of vision which
takes us as close as we can get to the truth. They are male
artists, these "big men," in the heroic mould, we may
infer, of a Michelangelo, battling "walls and faces of
massive stone." And they are perhaps the purest form of
artist, since their only audience is themselves and, presumably, the God who created human limitation in the
first place. Like workers in the realm of pure mathematics, they are obsessed with devising and carrying out of
perfect calculations. And yet in the evocation of that
violence over which MacLeod accords them mastery,
there is a reminder of the unspeakable danger to which
the miner is exposed in the performance of his art, unlike
mathematician or writer. And concomitant with that danger is the fact of the transitoriness of the work of art

produced – "which by its very nature cannot very long endure." But perhaps the epitome of the miners' dignity and superiority over engineers and lawyers and dentists lies in the fact that far from having been driven to a degrading and exploitative form of labour, they have "chosen" this occupation, and in the process transvalued and transformed it.

It is mining, rather that fishing or subsistence farming, that is the privileged form of labour – working art – in *No Great Mischief*. The *"clann Chalum Ruaidh"* miners epitomized by Calum, Alexander's oldest brother, are exiled from the home where they can no longer make a living, but like their compatriots in "The Closing Down of Summer," they are an elite team:

> As specialized drift and development miners, we worked on a series of short contracts with Renco Development. Although we were paid a fixed hourly wage, the various bonus clauses were what really interested us financially. We were paid by our footage and by how rapidly we progressed to the black uranium ore which waited for Renco Development and for us behind and beyond the walls of stone. In some ways we were like sports teams buoyed forward and upward by private agreements and bonuses based upon our own production. We worked mainly for ourselves, our victories and losses calculated within our individual and collective minds, and our knowledge of individual and collective contributions a shared and basic knowledge. (*NGM* 145-146)

The violence and danger sketched in "The Closing Down of Summer" – the narrator recalls the death in a Newfoundland mining accident of his younger brother, and the traumatic burial of the boy's body in Cape Breton soil – is shown full force in *No Great Mischief*. The very telling of the story of Calum's journey from elite miner to derelict drunk, the flashbacks to northern Ontario, moves the narrative forward and keeps a novel embracing so many reflections, concerns and stories, from collapsing under their accumulated weight. Although the novel quickly proceeds, after its opening chapter, to "the story of how [Alexander and his sister,] as three-year-old children, planned 'to spend the night' with [their] grandparents and remained instead for sixteen years until [they] left to go to university" (*NGM* 57), the dramatic heart of that story – the doomed walk out onto the ice, the mysterious drownings of the children's parents – takes up some thirty-nine pages of narration. For all its haunting power, this short-story-within-a-novel is displaced by what emerges as a rival, or at least contrasting narrative of legendary proportions. We might call it "the doom of Calum": his fall from grace, in order to defend the honour of his clan, his harsh period of penitential exile, and his long-delayed redemption, in the form of a permanent return to his homeland, to the dark earth of Cape Breton.

It is in Calum's return home, at the novel's end, in the dramatic journey through ice and snow and over perilous bridges, that the elegiac trajectory of MacLeod's novel is realized. The elegy is sung, not just for a brother, and not even for a heroic miner, but for a form of labour, an ethic and aesthetic of work which has vanished, and with it, the values and meanings that formed the very identity of the *clann Chalum Ruaidh* and others like it in the Maritimes. For after the death of Fern Picard, it seems that none of Calum's brothers return to mining: one becomes a school bus driver in British Columbia; another goes to live in Scotland and work on a fish farm with the descendants of his forebears. Alexander, of course, becomes an orthodontist, but he no longer sees himself "in [his] white coat with [his] dentist's drill as an extension of [his] earlier self, with the jackleg drill . . . Drilling deep but not too deep. Trying to get it right" (*NGM* 273).

MacLeod's elegy for the loss of a form of labour that has become both an ethos and an expression of that love, which, as he reminds us, makes all of us better (*NGM,* 272) becomes especially resonant in the context of the radical changes occurring in the economy of Atlantic Canada. Due to over-zealous exploitation of natural resources, industries such as mining and fishing are, as is well-known, in terminal decline. It is in the "knowledge industry" as defined by the new economy of cyberspace and telecommunications, that the region's economic salvation – or mere survival – would seem to lie. The narrator of *No Great Mischief,* whose profession represents, in the scheme of the book's values, the farthest possible remove from honest and authentic labour on land or sea, might well have been a computer consultant or CEO of Nortel, had this novel been set a decade or two later than it is. Orthodontistry may be, if MacLeod is to be believed, merely a matter of the cosmetic manipulation of appearance for deceptive purposes; computers deal with the manipulation of fast hits of "facts" rather than the arduous and ultimately tragic getting of wisdom. Yet whatever occupation is chosen to make the contrast between work of the brain and that of the hands, one thing is clear: the ecological devastation wreaked by factory fishing, the demise of the Maritime coal and steel industries and the technological revolution of the late twentieth century have rendered obsolete – antediluvian, almost – the way of living through labour, of rooting one's values and very identity, both personal and communal, in the honest and heroic work one performs, that *No Great Mischief* commemorates, rather than celebrates.

It is for this reason, I would argue, that the first and last chapters of MacLeod's novel bear witness to the lot of yet another group of displaced labourers, whose language and culture, like those of the exiled Cape Bretoners, marks them as foreign, but whose labour has an element of skill and artistry which reminds the reader of the mining "elite." I am referring, of course, to the migrant "contract" pickers – who live in impoverished and dingy conditions in order to make enough money, if they are lucky, to send home to their families:

> The Jamaicans and the Mexican Mennonites and the French Canadians move with dexterity and quiet speed. Their strong sure fingers close and release automatically even as their eyes are planning the next deft move. They do not bruise the fruit and their feet do not trample the branches or the vines . . . Many are in Canada on agricultural work permits and when the season is done they must make the long journey back to their homes . . . Some are on "nine-month" contracts allowing them to stay in Canada for a maximum of nine continuous months. If they stay longer they become eligible for Canada's social assistance and health programs. No one wishes them to become eligible for such programs except themselves. Sometimes, if they are in demand, they will leave the country for only a few days and then re-enter to begin another nine-month stay, or until they are no longer needed. Some have been following this pattern for

decades while their children are continents and
oceans away. They do not see their children or talk
to them very often. Neither they nor their children
ever visit the orthodontist. In the small houses in
which they temporarily live they sit, at the end of the
day, in their undershirts and on the edges of their
steel-rimmed beds . . . Sometimes they listen to music
on cassettes, the rhythm and the dialect and the language often being foreign and indiscernible to those
who pass by on the larger highways. Photographs sit
on orange crates or the scarred night tables. On Mon-
day morning when I smilingly greet my first patient,
the small houses will be empty and the men will, already, have spent long hours in the sun (*NGM* 169-
70).

Just as his novel suggests that nations are not defined by
arbitrary borders, but by a sharing, by often disparate
peoples, of the same weather, landscape, daily concerns
and sensitivities (*NGM* 247), so MacLeod insists upon a
transnational and transcultural solidarity among those
who perform authentic, necessary and demanding physical labour. There is an element here of that belief in the
saving grace of work asserted by Charlie Marlow in *Heart
of Darkness*, that seminal literary work of the beginning of
the twentieth century. It is significant that, at the end of
that century, MacLeod's novel should insist upon a Con-
radian vision of human solidarity, of that inclusiveness
and empathy which figures in its depiction of the migrant
contract pickers and, as well, in the brief reference to the
narrator's wife's childhood in "the hell of eastern
Europe." For all its Celtic soul, for all the Celtic crosses
and interlacings that decorate the novel's cover and its

text, *No Great Mischief* is a work that speaks across cultural and social borders, in the language of labour, and of love.

WORKS CITED

The Lost Salt Gift of Blood. Toronto: McClelland & Stewart, 1976.
As Birds Bring Forth the Sun. Toronto: McClelland & Stewart, 1986. (BBF)
No Great Mischief. Toronto: McClelland & Stewart, 1999. (NGM)

Lighthouse, Ring and Fountain

THE NEVER-ENDING CIRCLE IN
No Great Mischief

KARL E. JIRGENS

I turn to Calum once again. I reach for his cooling hand which lies on the seat beside him. I touch the Celtic ring. This is the man who carried me on his shoulders when I was three. Carried me across the ice from the island, but could never carry me back again. Out on the island the neglected fresh-water well pours forth its gift of sweetness into the whitened darkness of the night . . . Ferry the dead. *Fois do t'anam.* Peace to his soul . . . "All of us are better when we're loved." (283)

Against a background of half-remembered songs, stories, histories and legends, *No Great Mischief* laments the loss of family, identity and a Scottish heritage. The recursive narrative pattern, the hybrid of traditional oral form and post-modern structure, and the closing image of the Celtic ring suggest a cyclical and endless pattern of departure and return. The fresh-water well connotes the fountainhead of a cultural heritage that is sometimes obscured, at other times in danger of being forgotten, but always a source of inspiration. The juxtaposed well and ring serve as *leitmotifs* for this prize-winning novel.

The post-modern pattern of *No Great Mischief* signals

a departure from the more conventional structures of MacLeod's short stories. However, the topics in the novel and the stories are similar. Short story collections such as *The Lost Salt Gift of Blood*, and *As Birds Bring Forth the Sun* include many situational elements evident in the novel. Like the novel, the much anthologized title story to *The Lost Salt Gift of Blood* depicts a movement from the ordinary to the extraordinary, and shows how an unfortunate but natural occurrence can be transformed into legend. Both the short fiction and the novel are filled with images of flux, associated not only with the sea, but with mutability, represented by liquid, sperm, blood, perspiration, alcohol, and wind. This liquid world, mutable and chaotic, implies that life is as tentative as the shifting strand between land and ocean. Both novel and short stories juxtapose the death of parents with an island that floats isolated and distant within a confluence of mist and sea. The narrator's detached voice and unfixed memory complements this situation. The many animals, notably dogs and horses, underline connections with the past and the fluctuating natural world. Within the scope of this novel, MacLeod has the freedom to maneouver and shape the narrative in unprecedented and remarkable ways.

There is no conventional beginning, middle and end in *No Great Mischief*. The narrative is subject to the whims, omissions and embellishments of *"gille beag ruadh,"* or "the little red boy" as Alexander MacDonald is known. Perhaps above all else, this is a work of *memory*. The disjunctive and digressive narrative spun from the recollections of the middle-aged Alexander MacDonald, includes as many versions of the history of the *clann Chalum Ruaidh* as can be recalled. The pattern is associative rather

than linear, the disjunctive chronology spinning out episodes and leaving them, only to return. The cycle of
departure and return features intersecting views, jumps
in memory, leaps in perspective and shifts in voice. There
are recollections of the past, contemplations of the present, and projections into the future. Depictions are provi-
sional and sometimes incomplete. The past is articulated
through uncertainties, ellipses, conflicting histories, and
unresolved mysteries. The fates of some remain un-
known. Nor are all the recollections based on Alexander's
first-hand experiences. He admits that his tale is built
upon the recollections of others. Significantly, the final
words of the novel are not those of Alexander, but words
spoken by another, recalled by Alexander.

The voices of relatives, friends, enemies and others
emerge through Alexander's voice. This plurality of
voices or memories within Alexander's recollection establishes often-conflicting perspectives. Anglophones
are set against Francophones, Metis, Zulus, Eastern Euro-
peans, Caribbeans and others. Gaelic is set against English, and the sayings of the *clann Chalum Ruaidh* are set
against the rest of the world. The dislocated tongues,
voices and people haunt Alexander's memory. Embedded in this clan history are numerous cultural markers –
mottos, aphorisms, poems, songs, histories, and novels,
including Margaret Laurence's *The Diviners*, which also
addresses questions of a lost culture, and disappearing
language. Alexander confesses that the veracity of many
versions of the past is suspect, but knows that there are
few sources to draw from: "And if the older singers or
storytellers of the *clann Chalum Ruaidh*, the *seanaichies*, as
they were called, happened to be present they would

'remember' events from a Scotland which they had never seen, or see our future in the shadows of the flickering flames" (65). Alexander's comments about the process of re-telling lend the narrative a meta-fictional quality. This is as much a story about the creation of legend, as it is a tale about the MacDonald clan.

Post-modern literature has often been accused of being structurally innovative, but politically inconsequential. However, in *No Great Mischief*, political controversies are examined through politically charged re-readings of conventional history. As Grandfather MacDonald explains, conventional histories omitted the role of Scottish clans in events such the Franco-English conflict on the Plains of Abraham. The Grandfather's perspective, arguing against hegemonic histories, re-situates the clan's role in shaping Canada. Alexander's narrative scans a vast horizon that includes the clan's original departure from the hills of Scotland, its arrival in Cape Breton, the movement to the uranium mines of Elliot Lake, then the decrepit tenements of Toronto, onward to Alexander's office in Windsor, further to the sister's bungalow in Calgary, full circle back to Scotland with Catherine's visit, and finally back to Cape Breton with the death of Calum. The looping, never-ending circle of this vision, is like the illumination emanating from a great lighthouse, such as the one situated on the island home of Alexander's family, and akin to the pattern on Calum's traditional Celtic ring. And through the looping narrative cycle, and the recurring use of family names, the family is immortalized.

The narrative of *No Great Mischief*, with its voices within voices and recurring pattern of departure and return, finds a *leitmotif* in "the never-ending circle" of the Celtic ring. Alexander's American cousin (also named Alexander MacDonald), who comes to Canada as a draft-dodger during the Vietnam war, prompts the narrating Alexander to comment: "We noticed that he wore a Celtic ring upon his finger. The never-ending circle" (223). And at the close of the novel, when Calum dies, Alexander says: "I turn to Calum once again. I reach for his cooling hand which lies on the seat beside him. I touch the Celtic ring" (283). The pattern on the Celtic ring represents the flux of nature and being, as well as the inter-connected-ness of all life. The circling narrative participates in this flux by returning to the same points, but, each time with a slightly different perspective. The Celtic ring further represents the ongoing chain of existence which includes the spiritual, human, animal, vegetative, mineral and unformed worlds, linked in a cyclical continuum which regenerates itself within a shifting cosmology. The inter-stices in this pattern are indicative of transcendence, intersection, conjunction, communication, or separation, and feature the transitions of days, seasons, departures, returns, births, unions and deaths. The interstices also mark moments of inversion experienced by the displaced clan members, points where transcendental changes oc-cur. For example, the narrator's graduation coincides with the death of his clan relation and namesake, Alex-ander MacDonald. Soon after, the narrator takes his clan brother's place, working the mines in Elliot Lake. The never-ending circle is also a braid or knot that binds life and death, past and future. Through inversion, the cycle not only binds, but links and returns one to nature's rhythms as well as to one's ancestry.

Alexander's grandparents often said that "Blood is thicker than water." This connection binds him to his ancestral past and offers him the unique gift of heritage. Appropriately, the moment of focus on Calum's ring defines micro and macro-cosmic dimensions of a tribal identity confronting the temporal horizon. Memory is the device that addresses, retrieves, and orders this moving horizon.

The narrative winds in great sweeping loops that depart from and return to the points that changed and illuminated Alexander's life. These points feature a series of journeys and deaths, including great-great-great-grandparents Calum and Catherine, Alexander's grand-father's father, Alexander's parents and brother, the cousin Alex MacDonald in Elliot Lake, Alexander's brother Calum, and Fern Picard, Calum's rival. Each recalled telling or re-telling of a death by one of several characters, illuminates the life that was lost and the life that remains. Each repeated episode rekindles the family history, a lighthouse illuminating the past, present and future of the *clann Chalum Ruaidh*. Thus, Alexander serves in the traditional Celtic role of a "guardian of memory."

The stories and recollections within Alexander's memory create a meta-fictional and a meta-mnemonic work. In ancient myth, Mnemosyne, was the Titaness of memory, and the mother of the nine Muses who frequented the spring Castalia, which gave poetic inspiration, but was also linked to the river of the underworld. In ancient Celtic cosmology, the otherworld was an inscape, or an overlay, contiguous with the existing world, reached through specific crossing-places. The final juxta-

position of ferrying and fountain conjoins Eros and Tha-
natos, life and death.

Memory is the muse of this novel. Alexander has
tasted the waters of the fresh-water spring on the island
once occupied by his now-dead parents, and feels com-
pelled to tell and re-tell his tale. The flow of water from
the well, a manifestation of flux, aligns itself with rain,
tears, hair, salt water, alcohol, wind, conversation, language, song, blood, bodily fluids, and time itself. Further,
the spring-water arises out of mineral rock, an image in
counterpoint to flux and process. The rocky island, the
brick tenement slums of Toronto, the ancestral cairn atop
the cliff-side in Cape Breton, represent a relative stasis
which the erosive power of wind and water gradually
overcomes. Alexander and his brother Calum discuss
great-great-great-grandfather Calum's grave which
stands atop a Cape Breton cliff-side overlooking the
ocean:

> "I wonder if his grave is still there?"
> "Yes, but it is very near to the cliff's edge now. The
> point of land is wearing away. Some years faster than
> others, depending on the storms."
> "Yes, I imagine so," he says. "It was always so stormy
> there. It is almost as if his grave is moving out to sea,
> isn't it?" (11-12)

Even *Calum Ruadh*'s grave, mounted atop the rock cliff,
is eventually re-shaped by time. Rock, like memory,
eventually loses the battle for permanence.

In *No Great Mischief*, process and permanence, kinesis
and stasis are complemented almost cinematically by
angular, often stark illuminations – dusty tenement halls

lit by forty watt light-bulbs, shafts of September sun slanting through streaky windows, rainbow sprays of water splashed over bows of boats, lighthouse beams passing over craggy scarps. Images of seeing are fundamental to MacLeod's narrative. Fluctuations of light, water, sound and wind evoke a tentativeness, a condition of uncertainty that contrasts with the rocks of coastlines, the bricks of tenements, or the lost salt gifts of ancestral blood. Entropy and the erosion of physical presence allude to the disappearance of cultural heritage, group and collective memory, as well as personal and communal identity. The narrator's incomplete, half-forgotten story, gripping a portion of a disappearing past, yields an island-like sense of solitude.

While the looping narrative illuminates a broad horizon, the tale itself comes to a focus at the moment Alexander's brother dies. Alexander is aware that he has arrived at an important juncture. It is the end of the year, the end of the century, the end of the millennium, and the end of his brother's life (17). Alexander's own cultural heritage potentially faces a similar end, as shown by the American cousin who abandons the clan during a fatal battle in Elliot Lake. The clash of rock and liquid, stasis and kinesis, accentuates Alexander's struggle to recall a history that once seemed concrete or real, but over time, grew more evasive and unfixed. Such recollections can be lost altogether, unless guardians of memory – storytellers, songsters, poets – keep them alive. The narrator has no pretensions to authority. Instead, he recognizes an irony in the fact that he often embellishes or changes his story, thereby contributing to the erosion of perceptions of the past. Just prior to Catherine's discussion of disappearing language and lost ancestry, Alexander admits to projecting his thoughts onto the story of his family. As he leaves his alcoholic and dying brother in a Toronto tenement, he reveals that he is *imagining* Calum's thoughts:

> Through his sun-smudged window perhaps my brother sees Cape Breton's high hardwood hills. There the colours have already come to the leaves, and slashes of red and gold glow within the greenery and beneath the morning's mist. The fat deer move among the rotting, windfallen apples and the mackerel school towards the wind. At night one can hear the sound of the ocean as it nudges the land. Almost as if it is insistently pushing the land farther back. The sound is not of storm but rather one of patient persistence and it is not at all audible in the summer months. Yet now it is as rhythmical as the pulsing of the blood in its governance by the moon. (191-92)

The sun is important in this novel, but the moon moves the narrative just as it mobilizes tides and blood. Alexander's twin sister, Catherine recalls the fate of her great-great-great-grandmother, "never able to arrive at the new land nor get back to the old" (192). That grandmother, a young woman who left Scotland with Calum MacDonald, gave birth during the ocean voyage, died *en route* and was sewn into a canvas bag, then was dropped into the sea. She is aligned in youth with waxing moon, in prime of life with full moon, and in death with waning moon, an UR-mother embodying three facets of the life cycle. Catherine's recollection of the event shows a pattern of transition without closure. And Alexander's revelation of the fallibility of his memory and his tendency to embellish, to add, or to omit parts of the past, reveals that his

narrative is not so much about others, but about his *own*
perception, memory and imagination of others, fluctuations drawn from "imagination's mist" (26). While working in his office long after the Elliot Lake experience,
Alexander considers his recollections: "It is hard when
looking at the pasts of other people to understand the fine
points of their lives. It is difficult to know the exact
shadings of dates which were never written down and to
know the intricacies of events which we have not lived
through ourselves but only viewed from the distances of
time and space" (62). Alexander grips uncertain memory
with an anxious passion, blending fear of losing the past
with an ironic awareness that he holds more his own
imagining and projection, and less the past itself. He
cannot grasp the elusive *dinge an sich*, as Kant called it.
MacLeod seems less concerned with how representations
may conform to objects, and more concerned with how
objects may conform to the narrator's representations or
memories, a fictive posture that is arguably neo-Kantian.
Consequently, the *dinge an sich*, the forensic or actual
"truth" may be lost, but a greater *mythic* truth emerges
from the "imagination's mist." The many voices, tongues
and controversies speaking through Alexander's memory create a pattern that emulates the natural rhythms of
tides and seasons. And when the story of the clan is
integrated with macrocosmic rhythms, exaltation occurs.

At the end of the novel, the cyclical narrative pauses
to illuminate Calum's incomplete and impossible return
"home," incomplete because death intervenes, impossible because, once left behind, home can never be re-
gained. Home can no longer be Scotland, the place the
clann Chalum Ruaidh left when it migrated from Moidart

to Cape Breton generations ago. Home can no longer be
Cape Breton after so many years away. "Home" is not
merely a physical place, but a state of mind, a condition.
Within the looping narrative, Calum's death marks only
a transition, a momentary suspension. The cycle of departure and return can never be completed. This is an
immigrant tale of permanent displacement. Closure is
ontologically impossible because displacement is permanent.

But there is a consolation to this displacement. The
Gaelic language, songs, poetry, legends and histories that
emanate from the "lighthouse" of Alexander's narrative
provide a guide through the fog of time to a cultural
heritage partly lost, partly retrieved. When Alexander
MacDonald's parents died on the shifting Cape Breton
ice, one of two lanterns they were carrying was lost at sea,
signifying that which can never be retrieved. The other,
perhaps tossed up by one of the drowning parents, continued to burn on the floe, a focal point igniting Alexander's memory. Without some articulation of the past, this
second lantern might also be lost. As narrator, Alexander
assumes his place as guardian of the story of the *clann
Chalum Ruaidh*. And so, the never-ending circle of the
narrative emanates from a "little red boy" become light-
house-keeper.

Re-Sourcing the Historical Present

A POSTMODERN TURN IN ALISTAIR MACLEOD'S SHORT FICTION

COLIN NICHOLSON

As Clearance-driven emigration from historic Scotland's Highlands and Islands into Canada transmutes into economically pressurised out-migration from contemporary Nova Scotia, transitions from Gaelic to English regularly marked by the need to gloss surviving Celtic phrase and saying constitute textual equivalences for an ethnic displacement out of which Alistair MacLeod forges his fictions (Davidson 41). Imagined voices alert to the linguistic, cultural and ontological networks that construct their interactive environments also disclose, in the example of the university teacher who narrates "The Boat," inescapable contexts for scripted speech-acts: "I say this now with a sense of wonder at my own stupidity in thinking I was somehow free" (MacLeod 12). In the same story, a father already fifty-six years old at the time of the narrator's conception, thematises genealogy as a compressed and formative temporality where the surviving son's autonomy is problematised as a permanent mediation through prior representation. For Cape Breton communities produced by "Ireland's discontent and Scotland's Highland Clearances and America's War of

Independence" (3-4), writing in which the personal is always already historical articulates identity, conflict and relationship. Because MacLeod's narrators tell tales that unfold myths of origin connecting them with a Highland past, the collective unconscious of an imagined historical community significantly constructs present selfhood and landscape out of remembered event.

When the miner MacKinnon who narrates "The Closing Down of Summer" thinks of his mining gang as "Greek actors or mastodons of an earlier time. Soon to be replaced or else perhaps to be extinct" (225), he describes by implication Archibald, seventy-eight-year-old descendant of an immigrant who, in "The Tuning of Perfection," has "come to be regarded as 'the last of the authentic old-time Gaelic singers' and is still remembered as 'the man from Skye'" (229). Since his discovery by folklorists twenty years before the opening of the story Archibald has been repeatedly interviewed and written about in articles typically entitled "Cape Breton Singer: The Last of His Kind" (234-5). The Scottish folklorist Calum MacLean, brother of the Gaelic poet Sorley MacLean, spent a lifetime gathering and recording the songs and stories of domestic Gaeldom and produced in 1958 a Highland memoir that has a bearing on Archibald's place in MacLeod's Nova Scotian fiction:

> A new culture had penetrated the Rough Bounds (*Garbhchriochan*) of the Gael, and was sweeping before it all traces, all memories of the past. Before it became too late, I had to recover something that would give our contemporaries and the generations of the future some picture of that past. My sources of information were not to be guide-books, travellers' accounts or the prejudiced writings of formal histo-

rians. They had to be living sources breathing the air
and treading the soil of [the Highlands] . . . In the
past, generation after generation of them returned
slowly to the dust and left not one single record of
what they ever knew or learned about their *patria*.
Without doubt the transmission of knowledge had
proceeded orally for centuries . . . The process was
about to cease because the younger generation was
no longer interested in its continuance. The culture
of Hollywood has certainly influenced youth in [the
Highlands] today. (99)

Archibald has already passed into print: his appearance
on television would produce a further integration into
North American contemporaneity but entail a loss of
cultural and personal definition. The terms and tactics by
which MacLeod's self-identifying subjects relate their
constructed identities to imagined communities becomes
a significant part of what these stories are about, including Archibald's unwillingness or inability to change his
singing for performance in a medium organised by people who know little and care less about how Gaelic actually signifies.

So it seems fitting that "As Birds Bring Forth the Sun"
should explore in more detail the continuance of Gaelic
myth and legend into modern, metropolitan Canada. On
his travels around Scotland, Calum MacLean talked to a
shepherd in the mainland district of Morar, south of the
Isle of Skye, who laughed on being asked if he were afraid
of meeting the legendary Grey Dog of Meoble:

The Grey Dog of Meoble makes its appearance when
any one of the MacDonalds of Morar, the seed of
Dugald, is about to die. There are several people still

living who maintain that they have really seen the
mysterious dog . . . Over two hundred years ago a
MacDonald of Meoble had a grey hound. He had to
leave to take part in some campaign and at the time
of his leaving, the hound was in pup. When he left,
the bitch swam out to an island on Loch Morar and
there gave birth to a litter. Months went by and Mac-
Donald returned home again, but his greyhound was
missing. He happened to go to the very island where
the bitch had her litter. The pups had now grown up
into huge dogs, and not recognising their master, at-
tacked and killed him before the mother appeared on
the scene. Ever since that time the Grey Dog has appeared as an omen of death. (138)

Off the western coast of South Morar stands the Island of
Eigg which Alistair MacLeod's ancestors left for Cape
Breton in the 1790s, and by beginning the title story of his
second volume with the simplicity of "Once there was a
family with a Highland name who lived beside the sea,"
MacLeod makes regional identifications at once territori-
ally specific and mythically resonant. "And the man had
a dog of which he was very fond. She was large and grey,
a sort of staghound from another time" (134). Scottish
story surfaces in Canadian retelling which preserves
original narrative circumstance as well as the Gaelic *cù
mòr glas* – the big grey dog – and thereby harks back to
ancestral orality as it becomes the "big grey dog of death"
in metropolitan North American text. Each time a violent
death occurs in the family, the *cù mòr glas a' bhàis* is
ritually invoked. Since the first owner is our narrator's
great-great-great-grandfather, the legend is experienced
as a family affair. A genealogical fiction produces a fiction
of genealogy that has been internalised as self-definition:

"With succeeding generations it seemed the spectre had somehow come to stay and that it had become *ours* – not in the manner of an unwanted skeleton in the closet from a family's ancient past but more in the manner of something close to a genetic possibility" (144).

The story called "Island" concentrates themes of personal and linguistic survival and of cultural marginalisation in a study of isolation that also involves the origins and impulse of myth. Using patterns of repetition and return that characterise oral narratives, the writing rigorously presents experiential, climatic and environmental actuality, but filters them through the uncertain perception of a focalising protagonist. When Agnes first sees her lover from a kitchen window, "she wrapped the damp dish towel around her hand as if it were a bandage and then she as quickly unwrapped it again" (85), a gesture re-enacted in the different circumstances of the story's end. Repetition prevaricates temporality, interrogating sameness and difference across the passage of time. When altered circumstance challenges surviving modes of self-apprehension, "Island" blurs generic boundaries between realist study in the psychology of loneliness and ghost-story, exploring the effects of changed conditions on unchanging structures of belief and assumption. Desire and frustrated motherhood combine to shift realism towards fantasy; and imaginary relationships to determining conditions come to seem as fully determining as the material circumstances which stimulated the imaginings. When Agnes looks towards the mainland:

> Because of her failing sight and the nature of the weather she was not sure if she could really see it. But she had seen it in all weathers and over so many

> decades that the image of it was clearly in her mind,
> and whether she actually saw it or remembered it,
> now, seemed to make no difference. (79)

As discriminations between what is imagined and what
is perceived dissolve, specific threshold modifies into
uncertain hinterland while ontology becomes identified
through topography. "Gradually, with the passage of the
years, the family's name as well as their identity became
entwined with that of the island . . . As if in giving their
name to the island they had received its own lonely
designation in return" (83-4).

If writing has been considered from Plato onwards as
constituting a threat to the living presences of authentic
– spoken – language, in these Nova Scotian versions it
structures the necessary here and now for marginalised
subjectivities recording their own vanishing trace.
Macleod's speaking subjects are written as they insist that
they are saying, so that writing in this usage does not
"displace the *proper place* of the sentence, the unique time
of the sentence pronounced *hic et nunc* by an irreplaceable
subject," but becomes instead the only possible medium
of that irreplaceable subject's utterance (Derrida 281).
The return of the repressed is repeatedly figured as Gaelic
phrase and cadence in acts of narration paradoxically
concerned to preserve Celtic memory by transposing its
signifying systems into English. What then happens is
that the lucid constructions of single speaking subjects
cannot be reduced to an order of univocal (single-voiced)
truth. MacLeod's speakers make their language; but they
do not make it in contexts of their own choosing: precur-
sor forms constantly ghost concretely rendered self-pres-
ences whose evanescence is thereby indelibly inscribed.

Reconstructing a Christmas memory for his eleven-year-old self on a small farm on the west coast of Cape Breton is not easy for the adult, self-aware narrator of "To Everything There Is a Season":

> My family had been there for a long, long time and so it seemed had I. And much of that time seems like the proverbial yesterday. Yet when I speak on this Christmas 1977, I am not sure how much I speak with the voice of that time or how much in the voice of what I have since become. And I am not sure how many liberties I may be taking with the boy I think I was. For Christmas is a time of both past and present and often the two are imperfectly blended. As we step into its nowness we often look behind. (111)

Where it is impossible to remember the consciousness of childhood, it will be correspondingly inconceivable that cultural ancestry can be present in easily recoverable forms. MacLeod himself is living on the edges in this writing, probing a margin of thought and being where past and present blend a seeming contrast between myths of origin and the rigours of continuity. "How many thousands of days," asks Benedict Anderson, "passed between infancy and early adulthood vanish beyond direct recall! . . . Out of this estrangement comes a conception of personhood, *identity* . . . which, because it cannot be 'remembered,' must be narrated." Awareness of being embedded in secular, serial time: "with all its implications of continuity, yet of 'forgetting' the experience of this continuity . . . engenders the need for a narrative of 'identity'" (204-205). Embedding in serial time involves writing and that in turn leads vocal spontaneity into scripted record. The miner MacKinnon, while repeatedly emphasising speech and its difficulties – "It is difficult to explain . . ." (215); "We will not have much to say . . ." (219); "I would like to tell . . ." (219) – is unable to enter "deeply enough" into the significations of the Zulu dancing he witnessed in Africa. This narrator feels trapped in the prison-house of a language he deploys expertly to communicate his feelings. His vivid self-representation in English comes to haunt a narrative that is itself entombed: the reader is participating – as recurrently in these tales – in the singing silence of a generally suppressed confessional. MacKinnon's interior monologue is a mark both of isolation from his family and of his stoical attitude and stance towards a Gaeldom felt to be terminal in his immediate group. Underground, Gaelic is the preferred sound-world, but in this narration the submerged breaks surface to speak English with compelling fluency.

The different stories related in "Vision" endorse Walter Ong's suggestion that "in all the wonderful worlds that writing opens, the spoken word still resides and lives. Written texts all have to be related somehow, directly or indirectly, to the world of sound, the natural habitat of language, to yield their meanings . . . Writing can never dispense with orality." *Rhetorike*, "speech-art," originally referred to oral tactics and strategies, but became a product of writing when schematised in, for example, Aristotle's *Art of Rhetoric*, as an organised "art" or science. So from the beginning, it can be argued, writing did not reduce orality but enhanced it (Ong 8). But, typically, as MacLeod brings into focus the mode of production of story, the effect of story upon self, and the making of self through the making of story expose narrative identity as deferral. In these interactions on-going self-construction competes with already constructed versions of self. As ways of seeing and saying shape ways of being, blindness and insight come into contention: memory, self-definition and cultural derivation constitute subjectivity as process, in which origin is always duplicitous. "Vision" blends memory into continuity, speech into writing and story into creed, where our narrator's hold on the remembered story and on the circumstances of that remembering is as powerful as but no more powerful than the story's hold upon him. It is, moreover, not one story but several, so that univocality generates the plurality which makes single voices possible. This speaker is as much produced by other narratives as he is a producer of his own and these tensions are represented as physical pain in a collision between memory, cognition and imagined story. MacLeod's text weaves its patterns of repetition in ways that both sustain and entrap, and Walter Benjamin's reminder to us that *textum* originally signified web is relevant: "For an experienced event is finite – at any rate, confined to one area of experience; a remembered event is infinite, because it is only a key to everything that happened before it and after it" (202). Shifting configurations of space, time and selfhood involve the reader in unfixed boundaries between storied memory and myth, and between legend, history and genealogy, so that what we think we know at any given moment is subject to slippage. Reference is made to "a quoted story from the time" being recalled (145), and we are regaled by a story of uncertain provenance and insecure definition told by our narrator's friend Kenneth MacAllester when they were schoolboys, about his

grandmother's distant ancestor from Scotland, a man
with second sight (in the Gaelic given here *Da Shealladh*);
a telling that combines narrative indeterminacy with
compelling detail of recall. Existing in more than one
version, the legendary protagonist in this embedded tale
is himself uncertainly identified, being called either
MacKenzie or Munro (though "his first name was Kenneth"), who could see spatially distant synchronic events
as well as those of the future by looking through a hole
in a magical white stone. Prophetic in the particular sense
that it pre-scribes something that will subsequently happen to the teller of this tale, the eye that this legendary
prophet placed to the stone for his visions "was *cam* or
blind in the sense of ordinary sight." In the story as told
between the two boys walking home from school, mur-
derous violence also produces a prophecy concerning the
end of a family-line that would come about "when there
was a deaf-and-dumb father who would outlive his four
sons" (148). The two boys arrive home from school still
talking about this story and Kenneth's mother then produces Walter Scott's version of the tale, to which our
remembering narrator "did not pay much attention" although he can remember and quote lines which refer to
the father and his four doomed sons:

> Thy sons rose around thee in light and in love
> All a father could hope, all a friend could approve;
> What 'vails it the tale of thy sorrows to tell?
> In the springtime of youth and of promise they fell!
> (Scott 647-8)

Attention to the source of these lines helps to focus some

of the ways in which "Vision" prevaricates self-definition with myths of derivation.

Walter Scott's poem, "Farewell to Mackenzie, High Chief of Kintail" begins: "Farewell to Mackenneth, great Earl of the North," suggesting a link with the name of our remembering narrator's story-telling friend. Already written in 1810, the poem is dated 1815 and is described as being "From the Gaelic" and composed, as a prefatory note explains: "by the Family Bard upon the departure of the Earl of Seaforth, who was obliged to take refuge in Spain, after an unsuccessful effort at insurrection in favour of the Stuart family, in the year 1718." Scott's knowledge of Gaelic was tenuous at best, so the status of his translations – which he described as "Saxonising" – is not easily determinable (Grierson 398-9). But when the historical Francis Humberston Mackenzie died in 1815, having outlived four sons of high promise, his title died with him and Scott was prompted to write an additional six stanzas called an "Imitation of the Preceding Song" and publish the ten stanzas together. It is from these added lines that the MacLeod story-within-a-story quotes. The evidence suggests that Mackenzie lost his hearing at the age of twelve and he died, Scott records in a letter, with "all his fine faculties lost in paralytic imbecility" (Lockhart 18-19). Scott alludes to a prophecy dating from the time of Charles II according to which in the days of a deaf and dumb Caberfae (Gaelic name for the chief of the Mackenzie clan) the male line would come to an end. Whatever intertextual relationships we think we detect, we see through a glass darkly: Gaelic inscription commemorating failed political insurrection and consequent exile shifts almost one hundred years later into Scott's verses elegising the demise of a family's claim to clan leadership. As quoted in MacLeod's text, the tale is embellished with suspicions of sexual intrigue, second-sight prophecies and catastrophic revenge, which do not figure in earlier versions. Fact transmutes to fantasy in transitions from song to script, and fictions from time past and another country shape fictions closer to the present of this Nova Scotian immigrant community. We are returned to the now of the telling of the first remembered story by our narrator's father as he waits with his remembering son to unload their lobster catch at the end of the fishing season.

The remembered story begins with repeated concern about whether Canna Point can actually be seen at the moment of telling. In one of the tale's most persistent gestures, visibility and perception are at a premium. Named after the Hebridean island of Canna, "the green island" where most of its original settlers were born (149), it is also the birthplace of our narrator's grandmother. So memory, genealogy and story combine to produce contending senses of blindness and insight, of different locales, of continuity and discontinuity, of belonging and separation, of rootedness and exile over time and in specified space. But any grounding sense of place is destabilised in other ways: whereas an island called Canna is situated off the western coast of Scotland, there is no corresponding Canna Point in Nova Scotia – it is a fictional *topos* contributing to the blurring of boundaries between actually existing topography and the realia of fiction. Time also seems repeatedly to be dissolving in this text, from "that long-ago time" at the end of one paragraph to "about this time of year" at beginning of the

next and then to the present registration of "by that time"
and the discovery of letters "from another distant time"
followed by the past of "at that time" in the paragraph
which follows (149-50). The remembered story then fis-
sures – or seems to fissure – to allow space for a digression
about Syrian and Lebanese peddlers "in the early years
of the century" who would act as message carriers between isolated communities, prefiguring just such an act
of communication later in the remembered story. When
story prefigures story, both time and space become fluid
and metaleptically transferable. Introducing legend and
superstition about the Irish figure Columba cross-fertil-
ises myth with a supposed initiating encounter between
Celtic Christianity and Gaeldom in the Scottish Highlands; and in "Vision" belief departs from evidence, and
faith joins hands with fantasy to produce again a process
of fleeting metalepsis, at once serial, circular and overlapping. Legend encrusting around Columba offers a bewil-
dering variety of possibilities from which 'Vision' selects
and constructs its particular preferences; thereby bringing into question the status of event of record in relation
to the inventive power of recording narrative. The grandfather's story to two children on the fictional locale of
Canna Point includes English language translations of
verses from an anonymous twelfth-century Irish poem
whose words are put into the mouth of a Columba reflect-
ing upon his banishment:

> There is a grey eye
> Looking back on Ireland,
> That will never see again
> Her men or her women.

> Early and late my lamentation,
> Alas, the journey I am making;
> This will be my secret bye-name
> "Back turned on Ireland." (162)

Again exile's desiring gaze and again the impossibility of actual return. We are in realms where Celtic twilight stretches back to thickest fog and where a maze of more or less improbable legends composes a scripted territory where fairy-tale and faith intersect. The possible battle in which Columba may have fought and to which the grandfather in "Vision" refers, has been read as representing strife between Christian and Druid and, deriving as they do from an era when anything was conceivable if it came dressed in the language of the miraculous, the interpretative possibilities of these remembered episodes and events begin to appear limitless. But in the tissue of visions, prophecies and predictions encountered in the early stages of developing Celtic belief-systems relating to Columba and a Christianising drift from Ireland to Scotland, the attribution to him of *Da Shealladh*, the second sight, and the claim that he, too, "used a stone to 'see' his visions" (161), is seemingly the invention of the story-telling grandfather in MacLeod's tale: an encryption of myth as accretions of memory and circlings of narrative that interpellates the reader as participant observer in processes of fictionalisation where language enshrines event in preferred forms, writing embalms memory and the text traces myth in the making. The survival of myth as potent repository for individual and ethnic identity and continuity is rehearsed when the listening children ask their story-telling grandfather whether he knew Columba: "sometimes I feel I know him and I think I see him as well" (162). We begin to understand Michel Foucault's impatience with the construing faith of those who wish for a secret origin beyond any apparent beginning: "so secret and fundamental that it can never be quite grasped in itself. Thus one is led inevitably, through the naiveté of chronologies, towards an ever-receding point that is never itself present in any history; this point is merely is its own void" (25). If the coming of Columba to what is now known as Scotland signifies an extended historical moment of the grafting of Christian sign and ritual onto pagan precedent, in the grandfather's reference to the Scottish diaspora when inhabitants of "the green isle" were scattered "all over the world," we read subsequent survivals of related structures of self-perception: "But some of us are here. That is why this place is called Canna and we carry certain things within us" (163). "Here" is a fictional inscription and no equivalencies are easy in this writing.

"Vision" allegorises cultural derivation. As time passes and memory is activated for the two boys now returned to their home in Kintail (also a real Scottish place fictively transposed to Cape Breton): "the details blended in with their own experience . . . they could see the fire . . . sometimes they imagined her . . . they heard her call in their imagination and in their dreams." These dreams then become a shared experience in which they hear the blind woman calling 'Co a Th'ann? . . . Who's there? And one night they dreamed they heard themselves answer. "Se mi-fhin" they heard themselves say with one voice. It is myself" (167): dream-state self-identifications constitute self-definition. "Vision" is similarly produced on the page as a text our remembering narrator half creates and half receives: "This, I guess, is my retelling of the story told by the young man of Canna to my father and his brother at a time when they were young and on the verge of war . . . The story was told in Gaelic, and as the people say, 'It is not the same in English,' although the images are true" (172). And when we are subsequently told that the grandfather from Canna, *Mac an Amharuis*, the son of uncertainty, died aged more than one hundred, unable to recognise, either by sight or sound, any of the people around him, we glide back intertextually to Walter Scott's Chief of Kintail dying in not dissimilar circumstances, though "Vision" does not disclose this information on its own narrative surfaces. Fiction articulates with fiction, narrative copulates with memory, legend coalesces with genealogy:

> When I began this story I was recounting the story which my father told to me as he faced the green hills of Canna on the last day of the lobster season a long time ago. But when I look on it now I realise that all of it did not come from him, exactly as I have told it, on that day. (173)

"Vision" is a supple enactment in fiction of the overlapping and ultimately inseparable procedures of recall by which history encrusts into legend, legend shades into myth and remembered story imbricates speaking selves; origins retreat into different tellings, and subjectivity derives from hybridising intertexts: "This has been the telling of a story about a story but like most stories it has spun off into others and relied on others and perhaps no story ever really stands alone" (177). "To tell a story," Alessandro Portelli points out, "is to take arms against the threat of time . . . the telling of a story preserves the teller from oblivion . . . Time is one of the essential things stories are about" (Tonkin 3). As MacLeod's narrators talk of a past, they reveal a shaped and shaping continuity that figures ontological entrapment for speakers who are as much shaped as shaping because the first-person narratives they utter are intertextual derivations from prior story.

WORKS CITED

Anderson, Benedict. *Imagined Communities: Reflections on the Origin and Spread of Nationalism*. London: Verso, rev. ed., 1991.

Benjamin, Walter. "The Image of Proust." *Illuminations: Essays and Reflections*. Trans. Harry Zohn. New York: 1968.

Davidson, Arnold. "As Birds Bring Forth the Story: The Elusive Art of Alistair MacLeod." *Canadian Literature* 119 (Winter, 1988).

Derrida, Jacques. *Of Grammatology* (1967). Trans. Gayatri Chakravorty Spivak. Baltimore: Johns Hopkins University Press, 1976.

Grierson, H. J. C., ed. *Letters of Sir Walter Scott*. Vol. 2: 1808-11. London: 1932.

Foucault, Michel. *The Archaeology of Knowledge*. London: 1972.

Lockhart, J. G. *Life of Sir Walter Scott*. Vol v. Edinburgh: 1839.

MacLean, Calum I. *The Highlands*. Edinburgh: 1990.

MacLeod, Alistair. *The Lost Salt Gift of Blood: Collected Stories*. London: 1991.

Ong, Walter J. *Orality and Literacy: The Technologizing of the Word*. London: 1982.

Scott, Sir Walter. *Poetical Works*. Edinburgh: 1849.

Tonkin, Elizabeth. *Narrating Our Pasts: The Social Construction of Oral History*. Cambridge: 1992.

Alligators in the Sewers

PUBLISHING ALISTAIR MACLEOD

DOUGLAS GIBSON

Modern urban legends spring out of everywhere and nowhere. We all know for a fact that a cement truck operator avenged himself on the man who was dallying with the trucker's wife by filling his Mercedes with wet cement. And we thrill to the knowledge that some of our cities now have a flourishing alligator population deep in the warm sewers, the offspring of little baby gators flushed away by bored owners unaware of the subterranean monsters they were creating.

Alistair MacLeod and I have been living in the midst of just such an urban myth. As it spins more wildly out of control, we compare notes, bemused by the directions the myth takes, aware that we seem to be in the grip of something bigger than both of us. The once-simple story of how I encouraged Alistair to finish the novel that became *No Great Mischief* has taken the following turns. In Nova Scotia local legend has me flying to Halifax then driving to Cape Breton (soon, presumably, it will be in a storm, with the closed Canso causeway, under water, proving no obstacle to the wild-eyed publisher) and then rushing on foot to Alistair's writing cabin to wrest the manuscript from his grasp. Even in Ontario, the range of

stories can make a reader dizzy. Sometimes the manuscript is exchanged for a bottle of whiskey in Union
Station. Sometimes the exciting new versions involve my
driving to Windsor, dashing into the office of Professor
MacLeod and grabbing a manuscript written by hand on
exam paper notebooks. Best of all is the story first aired
in the *National Post* and then passed along by the *Edmonton Journal* – a story very popular in the halls of McClelland & Stewart – where the delivery of the manuscript's
final chapter at the M&S office causes me to burst into
tears of relief.

Alistair has perfected the art of being non-committal
about such stories, perhaps a legacy of his years as a
creative writing teacher reluctant to stamp out any fictional spark. Presumably by the time this account sees the
light of day the legend will have expanded in other
directions, possibly involving parachutes and guns.

The true story is as follows. Alistair published both
his short story collections *The Lost Salt Gift of Blood* (1976)
and *As Birds Bring Forth the Sun* (1986) with McClelland
& Stewart. I became M&S's Publisher in 1988, but of
course knew Alistair's work. Indeed, I had got to know
him in person at the Banff Centre where he worked as a
much-admired teacher in the summer with W. O.
Mitchell's creative writing programme (itself the source
of many stories, not least Alistair's side-splitting account
of his winter trip by taxi with W. O. from Calgary to
Banff.) And one summer in the mid-1980s, when the
Gibson family was touring the Maritimes, we visited the
MacLeods in Dunvegan. Between juvenile soccer games
on the grass in front of the house, Alistair showed us
around his corner of Cape Breton and I remember walk-

ing that grassy track to his spartan cliff-top writing cabin, which faces west to Prince Edward Island. It struck me at the time that, with the sound of the wind and the waves and the constantly changing view, I would get very little writing done there.

As McClelland & Stewart's Publisher I was in the happy position of having inherited Alistair, and so from 1988 was appropriately interested in how his work was coming along. Over the years, as it became clear that the work he had started in 1986 was a novel, and as Alistair's readings from the novel at events across the country produced a groundswell of excitement, my contact would consist of a cheery phone call every six months or so, asking how the writing was going. This would produce charmingly vague responses from the Windsor (or, in summer, the Cape Breton) end of the line. So vague, in fact, that I would rely on information from a friend in the M&S warehouse, a member of Alistair's extended family, for reports on his progress. There were many other friends and admirers, "MacLeod-watchers" (like Kremlin-watchers in the old days who would read significance into the arrangements of Soviet officials on a reviewing stand), who would pass on scraps of information about what he had read at this event, or mentioned about his manuscript in that interview or meeting.

All the while, of course, Alistair was holding down a demanding job teaching English and Creative Writing at Windsor (to the great benefit of his appreciative students), teaching a summer course at Banff, and raising six children with Anita, not to mention undertaking annual family moves between Windsor and Cape Breton. So I did not feel able to harass the man beyond the point of regular encouraging phone calls, letting him know that there was continuing interest at M&S, and in the wider world, in his next book.

This changed around the beginning of 1999. All of my "how's it coming along" questions – which Alistair has accurately likened to the "are we there yet?" questions from the kids in the back seat on a long car trip – had extracted no hard information about what proportion of the manuscript was now written. The book, despite my repeated offers, was still not under contract, presumably because Alistair was reluctant to commit to a specific delivery. But messages from the "MacLeod-watchers" and my own sense of his situation led me to step up the pressure. My main motive was commercial. I could see that very few of the major figures in Canadian literature would have a new book in the fall of 1999 – Alice Munro had appeared the previous year, Margaret Atwood, Michael Ondaatje, Rohinton Mistry and Jane Urquhart, among others, were not due for another year at least – so a book by a respected but not widely-known author like Alistair MacLeod would have a chance to rise to the top, would have, to change the metaphor, room to breathe.

So my phone calls became more frequent, and more urgent, especially after Alistair rashly allowed that it was possible that he might finish the book in time for fall publication. I have referred to him as a stone-carver, chipping out each perfect word with loving care. Certainly my confidence in the excellence of his writing was such that – without having read a word of the manuscript – I felt able to put the book in the Fall 1999 catalogue (going to the printer at the end of May) and to write him a letter in April outlining very precisely the generous terms we would offer for the new book, for which we would hold "a place of honour" in our fall list.

In the midst of this campaign of harassment, I learned that Alistair would be reading in Toronto. Unluckily, I had a previous engagement in Ottawa at the opening of a James Houston-inspired show of Inuit Art at the Museum of Civilization that same evening. But the next day I flew back early from Ottawa, and called Anita in Windsor to announce that I really wanted to see her husband while he was in Toronto. She told me where he was staying and mentioned that he was catching the 4:30 train back to Windsor. Failing to catch him before he checked out, I decided, with our Chairman Avie Bennett's amused encouragement, to try a direct approach.

So it came about that the unfortunate Dr. MacLeod, peacefully reading a book in Union Station at 4:00 o'clock, found a bearded man in a coat dropping down to sit beside him on the bench with the words: "Isn't this amazing! Here I am patrolling Union Station in search of a best-selling novel for this fall, and I happen to run into you!"

We laughed, but I was able to emphasize the urgency of the matter, in person, and to tell him how certain I was that the literary world was eagerly awaiting this book (something that Alistair, a truly modest man, found hard to believe, even though I assured him that I was right on this.) Above all, I was able to urge him on to a final sprint as he approached the finish line of this long distance race. Alistair was politely non-committal. When the Windsor train was called and a queue began to form there was a fine moment when I offered to carry his briefcase, with a look of frank, open-hearted generosity, and Alistair laughed and clutched the bag protectively to his chest. Laughing, but still clutching.

To keep the pressure on, I put the book in the M&S catalogue, writing a description of the novel that stands up remarkably well, given that I had not yet read a word of it, or learned more than a sentence or two about it from the tight lips of the author. (When the manuscript later came in, containing the two lines of poetry that immediately preceded the two lines I had chosen to quote in the catalogue, I knew that the gods were with us.)

At this point the title changed. It had originally been *No Great Mischief If They Fall*, but Alistair phoned to report that he had just learned of a Scottish book with the same title. Not necessarily a problem, I said, since titles are not restricted by copyright. "Ah well," said Alistair, "unfortunately, the name of the other book's author is MacLeod." In one second the book became *No Great Mischief*, as nature surely intended.

As we neared the end of May the pressure on both of us increased. The catalogue was about to be printed at the end of the month, and it is not good for a book to be announced and then postponed. My phone calls about needing to see the manuscript by mid-May were not bearing fruit. Finally, on a Wednesday I called Windsor to tell Alistair that, because we were nearing catalogue deadline and because our sales conference was the following Tuesday and I could not face 40 or 50 people and describe the merits of a book I had not read, I was flying down to Windsor on Friday to pick up the manuscript.

He was appalled. No, no, it wasn't ready, I shouldn't do that, and so on. But I told him that I was coming, hung up, and didn't answer my phone for two days. (At the airport on Friday morning, while my office was calling Alistair to let him know I was indeed on my way, I ran into Heather Robertson, the well-known author, who asked where I was going and was fascinated to hear about my mission. One year later Heather was to be part of the jury that unanimously gave the Trillium Prize to *No Great Mischief*.) Arriving in Windsor, I startled the cab driver by asking to be taken to the nearest liquor store. He swung around nervously, checking for indications that I would pass out, or worse, throw up, on his back seat. Then, armed with a bottle of Talisker, a fine malt from the appropriate part of the Highlands, I went on to the MacLeod house.

At the door, I received a courteous but reserved reception from Alistair, and I was glad to have the Talisker to present. And we sat in the front room with Anita and chatted for a bit about our families, and it was very pleasant. But there was an elephant in the room that we were all ignoring. After all, I had barged into their lives with the express intention of wresting the manuscript out of his hands. To make matters worse, no manuscript was in view. Much worse, above the piano I could see the MacLeod clan coat of arms with its terrible, blood-chilling motto: "Hold fast."

I did not comment on this.

Eventually, I produced a contract for the book and laid the large envelope on the coffee table, noting that they should treat it with care because it also contained a cheque, and then wondered aloud what he had for me. And Alistair rose in silence and left the room – *and came back carrying a manuscript!* Needless to say, it never left my possession from that moment until I was back in

Toronto, jubilant from having read a wonderful piece of literature.

But not, it proved, a complete one. After Alistair had taken me to lunch downtown (and significantly he was greeted in the parking lot, *and* outside the restaurant *and* by another diner in the restaurant) and told me about the book's plot for the first time, he drove me to his office at the University. I noticed many hand-written scraps of paper. In response to my question, Alistair admitted that he wrote long-hand and the absence of secretarial help in summer vacation time meant that his final chapters were being held up while he asked others to type it for him as a favour. I reeled at the thought of this bottleneck and promptly arranged for him to send his remaining hand-written chapters to us by courier and we would arrange to get them typed and on a disc.

And so, for the next six weeks or so, a package of 10 or 12 or 15 pages written by hand on yellow paper would arrive every few days at the M&S office, and I would take it for typesetting to two young interns, Medbh Bidwell and Adrienne Guthrie, graduates of the Simon Fraser University Masters programme in publishing. They were initially a little hesitant about this menial typing assignment, although I assured them that they were playing a role in Canadian literary history: they soon came to agree, as their wonder at the material they were typing grew, along with their impatience to find out what happened next. My reaction to the final chapter was misunderstood by the *National Post* and the *Edmonton Journal* but will be easily grasped by anyone who reads the book and its last line: "All of us are better when we are loved." I was moved to tears.

My role in editing the book was almost non-existent. The early material, typed in a variety of faces over the years, was so polished that it needed almost no attention from me. Alistair's style is distinctive – sparse punctuation, a frequent preference for "which" instead of "that," much use of "perhaps," and dialogue punctuated very simply by "he said" so that a variant like "expostulated" would bring the whole chapter crashing down – and it is so deliberate and the rhythms so clear that pages of the manuscript would fly by untouched by editorial hand.

On occasion my own Scottish background (I was born and raised there, leaving St. Andrews University with a scholarship that took me across the Atlantic) proved to be very useful. For example, I knew a lot about Montrose's rebellion, having played the role of Montrose in a St. Andrews' procession – cavalier's hat, breastplate, sword, thigh-boots and all (not to mention the runaway horse) – so I was able to clarify the odd historical detail. By way of general helpfulness I was able, for example, to remind Alistair of Eliot's lines about Rannoch Moor when he was describing that area, and I was sound in the general area of Scottish history and, by extension, the battles at Beauport and upstream on the Plains of Abraham. (And if you shake your head at the ubiquity of Scots in Canada, consider that the aforementioned Abraham was "Abraham Martin, dit l'Ecossais.")

Another Scottish aside: Rannoch Moor is where Alan Breck Stewart and David Balfour spent a hot day being hunted by English redcoats in *Kidnapped.* Robert Louis Stevenson, who knew something about Jekyll and Hyde personalities, has been credited with making these two characters represent the two sides of what might be called the Scottish schizophrenic personality: David, the sober, plodding, industrious common-sense Presbyterian Lowlander (good material for lawyers, bankers, engineers and doctors), and Alan Breck, the wild, creative, romantic Highlander, an ideal man to set up a new fur trade route, to conquer a kingdom, to cry over a sad song or to fight in wars around the world. Working with Alistair – a Highlander to the bone – it was hard not to find myself being tugged into the ethnic role of my Lowland ancestors. In terms of the historic events of the book, these ancient Gibsons were presumably all in favour of Bruce (another Ayrshire man) and Bannockburn, where they were on the same side as the MacDonalds; but they were opposed to Montrose, dead set against "Bonnie Dundee" ("Bloody Claverhouse") at Killiecrankie, and notably unenthusiastic about Bonnie Prince Charlie. Now, centuries later and a world away, here I was, David Balfour-like, urging the commercial advantages of finishing a novel like a sober man of business, on Alistair, a Celtic visionary and a great artist. It was, and is, a sobering thought.

Understandably, I was useless as an editor when it came to Gaelic. A toast, a greeting, a few swear words, enough topographical features to be able to tell a Ben from a Loch, that was the extent of my knowledge, although I grew up in an Ayrshire village with a Gaelic name. So I called on the assistance of a husband and wife team from Scotland, now in Toronto, and they raised a number of proof-reading questions that Anita (the expert in the household) was able to settle. By the end I was familiar enough with the language that, to my great satisfaction, I caught a typo in the Gaelic dedication.

The expert copy-editor, Heather Sangster, main-

tained the same light-handed editorial approach, recognizing that the deliberately oral way of story-telling
adopted by the author right from the start ("as most
people hearing this will know" – page 3) called for deliberate repetition of certain phrases, such as "the modern-
istic house in Calgary." As always, such a skilled
copy-editor caught inconsistencies that had somehow
escaped the eyes of both author and editor over many
readings.

In terms of the text, my chief role was to work with
the designer to produce a book page that did justice to
the writing. The typeface is clean, traditional and easy to
read, with plenty of "leading" space between lines. There
are 43 chapters in the 283 pages of *No Great Mischief* so to
start each new chapter on a fresh page would be disrup-
tive to the reader's eye and would make the book seem
padded. Hence our decision to allow a six-line spacing
between chapters, and to mark each chapter opening
simply with a numeral set against a Celtic design.

The book was not divided into formal chapters when
it came to my office. I consulted Alistair by phone and
undertook to divide it into chapters as seemed best to me,
with occasional one-line breaks in the middle of a chapter
when something less than a full chapter break seemed
appropriate (see page 181, for one example). I am happy
to report that when we first saw the proofs of the book,
formally divided into chapters, Alistair and I agreed that
I had got it right the first time, with the exception of one
paragraph, which was moved back into the preceding
chapter.

After that it was merely a matter of giving the book
an appropriate look, which our Kong Njo, in his role as

Art Director, did with his usual skill (tactfully ignoring my suggestion that the MacDonald tartan might show up somewhere on the cover. Incidentally, at a Cape Breton launch for the book, the hall was decorated in MacLeod and MacDonald tartans, not to mention variants of the McClelland and the Stewart tartans. Had this particular Gibson been able to be present, the Buchanan tartan might also have put in an appearance).

In the course of presenting the book to our Sales Conference, that famous conference in June 1999, I did something unprecedented. I used music to convey the sense of the book. To be precise, from my "Puirt à Baroque" recording, I played "Niel Gow's Lament" in the background while I talked about how the music of the Scottish Highlands and of Cape Breton pervades this marvellous book. And the sad, slow music of the fiddle was worth a thousand words.

The publishing success of *No Great Mischief* is history, and it is history that is being written around the world, with publishers in a dozen other countries engaged in revealing the wonders of the book to their readers. A special pleasure for me was seeing the success of *No Great Mischief* as early as October and consequently urging Alistair to let us publish his collected short stories in the spring. There have been very few criticisms of any aspect of the novel but some critics have complained that the dialogue in Alistair's work does not sound realistic to their ears. My reply is that they have never talked much with Alistair MacLeod.

As far as I can reconstruct it, the conversation went as follows:

"Alistair," I said. "Would you have any other stories besides the fourteen that are in the two story collections?"

"Yes," he said, "I would."

"And how many do you have?"

"I have two," he said.

"And what are their names?"

"One is called 'Island,' he said, "and the other is called 'Clearances.'"

"And are they short or long?"

"Oh, they are both quite long."

"Well," I said, "in the spring I think we will bring out a book of your collected stories and we will call it either 'Island' or 'Clearances,' and we will do very well with it."

"Do you think so?"

"Oh yes," I said. "And I have been right before."

And we both laughed.

Biography

Alistair MacLeod was born in North Battleford, Saskatch-ewan, in 1936 and raised among an extended family in Cape Breton, Nova Scotia. He still spends his summers in Inverness County, writing in a clifftop cabin looking west towards Prince Edward Island. In his early years, to finance his education, he worked as a logger, a miner, and a fisherman, and writes vividly and sympathetically about such work.

His early studies were at the Nova Scotia Teachers College, St. Francis Xavier, the University of New Bruns-wick and Notre Dame, were he took his Ph.D. He has also taught creative writing at the University of Indiana. Working alongside W. O. Mitchell, he was an inspiring teacher to generations of writers at The Banff Centre. In the spring of 2000, Dr. MacLeod retired from the Univer-sity of Windsor, Ontario, where he was a professor of English.

In 1999, Dr. MacLeod published his first novel, *No Great Mischief* to critical acclaim. This book won The Dartmouth Book Award for Fiction, The Raddall Award for Fiction, The Trillium Award for Fiction, The CAA-MOSAID Technologies Inc. Award for Fiction. At the Canadian Booksellers Association Libris Awards, Dr. MacLeod won for Fiction Book of the Year and Author of the Year. In 2001, *No Great Mischief* won the International IMPAC Dublin Literary Award.

Dr. MacLeod and his wife, Anita, have six children. They live in Windsor.

Bibliography

MacLeod, Alistair. *The Lost Salt Gift of Blood*. Toronto: McClelland &
    Stewart, 1976.
As Birds Bring Forth the Sun and Other Stories. Toronto: McClelland
    & Stewart, 1986.
No Great Mischief. Toronto: McClelland & Stewart, 1999.
Island: The Collected Short Stories. Toronto: McClelland & Stewart,
    2000.

Contributors

Born in Scotland, educated at St. Andrews and Yale, Douglas Gibson came to Canada in 1967 and joined the publishing world in 1968. He joined McClelland & Stewart in 1986, becomes overall Publisher in 1988 and President and Publisher in July 2000. Over the years, he has worked closely with writers such as Hugh MacLennan, Robertson Davies, Alice Munro, W. O. Mitchell, Pierre Elliott Trudeau and Alistair MacLeod.

Irene Guilford, who has a degree in Mathematics and Computer Science, published her first novel, *The Embrace,* with Guernica. She lives in Toronto.

Karl Jirgens writes fiction, literary criticism, and edits the international literary journal Rampike. He is Associate Professor of English at Algoma University College, Laurentian University.

Poet and prose writer Janice Kulyk Keefer teaches at the University of Guelph and lives in Toronto. Her latest book is *Marrying the Sea.*

Colin Nicholson is Professor of Eighteenth-Century and Modern Literature at the University of Edinburgh. For the past ten years he was editor of the *British Journal of Canadian Studies,* during which time he edited collections of essays on Margaret Laurence and on Margaret Atwood.

Shelagh Rogers is the host of *CBC Radio One's This Morning.* A fervent admirer of Alistair Macleod since reading *As Birds Bring Forth the Sun,* she has been an addict since the first line.

Jane Urquhart, who has written six books of fiction and four books of poetry, has won the Governor General's Award, the Trillium Award, Le prix du meilleur livre étranger in France, the Marian Engel Award, and has been named a Chevalier dans

L'Ordre des Arts et des Lettres in France. She lives outside Toronto.

David Williams is Professor of English at the University of Manitoba, and the author of three novels and three books of literary criticism.